FOR ORGANS, PIANOS & ELECTRONIC KEYBOARDS

E-Z PLAY TODAY

260

MISTER ROGERS SONGBOOK

T0105928

ISBN 978-1-5400-4012-1

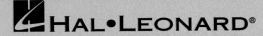

E-Z Play® Today Music Notation © 1975 by HAL LEONARD LLC
E-Z PLAY and EASY ELECTRONIC KEYBOARD MUSIC are registered trademarks of HAL LEONARD LLC.

Visit Hal Leonard Online at
www.halleonard.com

Contact Us:
Hal Leonard
7777 West Bluemound Road
Milwaukee, WI 53213
Email: info@halleonard.com

In Europe contact:
Hal Leonard Europe Limited
42 Wigmore Street
Marylebone, London, W1U 2RN
Email: info@halleonardeurope.com

In Australia contact:
Hal Leonard Australia Pty. Ltd.
4 Lentara Court
Cheltenham, Victoria, 3192 Australia
Email: info@halleonard.com.au

Are You Brave?

Registration 1
Rhythm: 8-Beat or Pops

Words and Music by
Fred Rogers

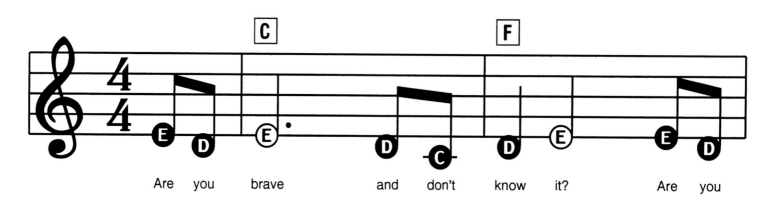

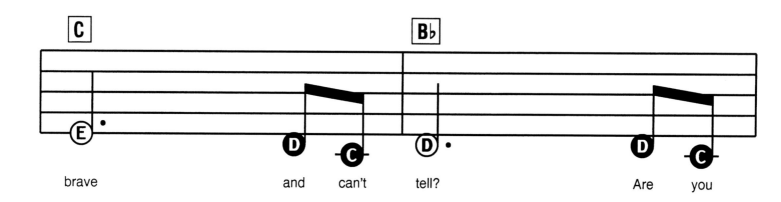

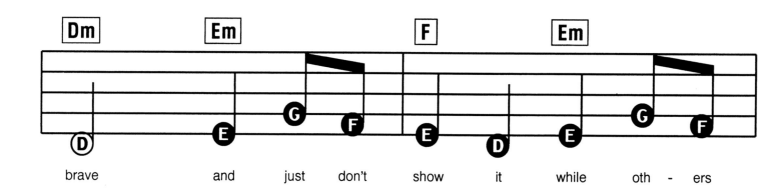

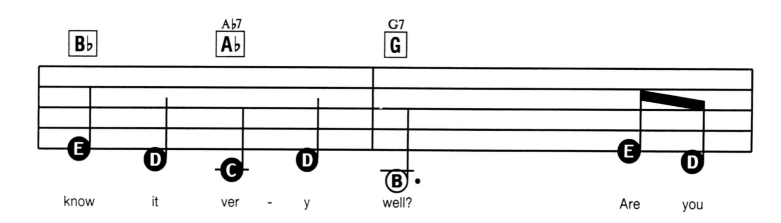

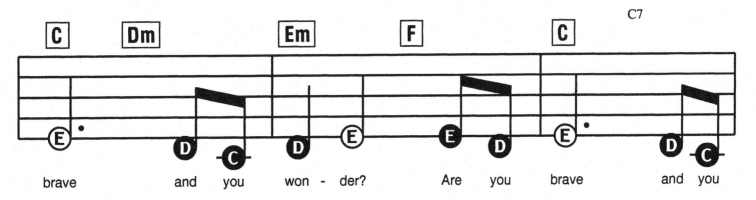

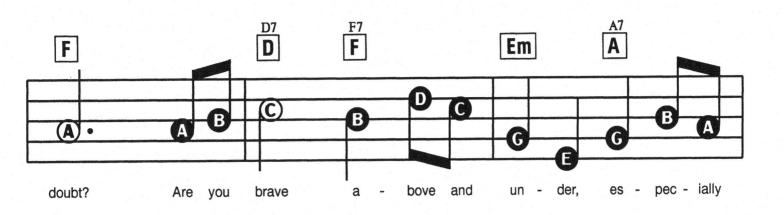

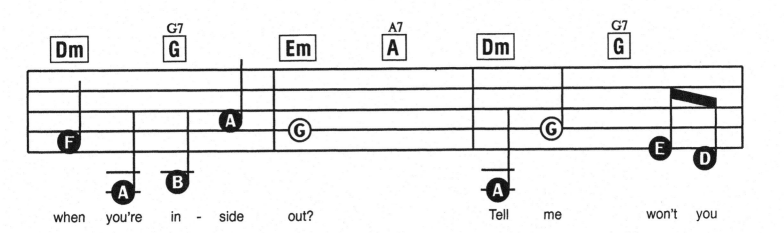

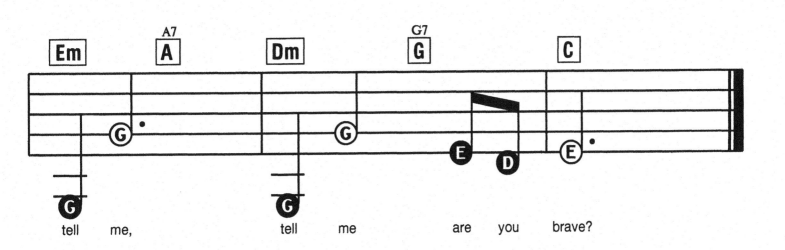

Days of the Week

Registration 8
Rhythm: Pops or Rock

Words and Music by
Fred Rogers

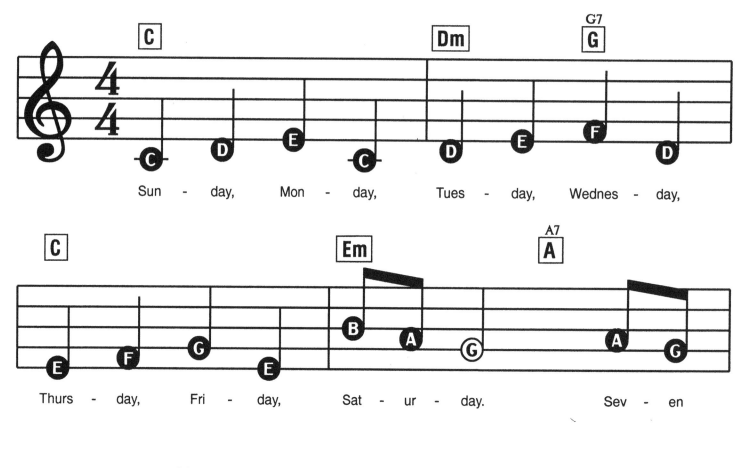

Sun - day, Mon - day, Tues - day, Wednes - day,

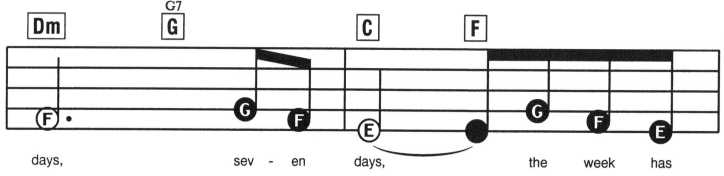

Thurs - day, Fri - day, Sat - ur - day. Sev - en

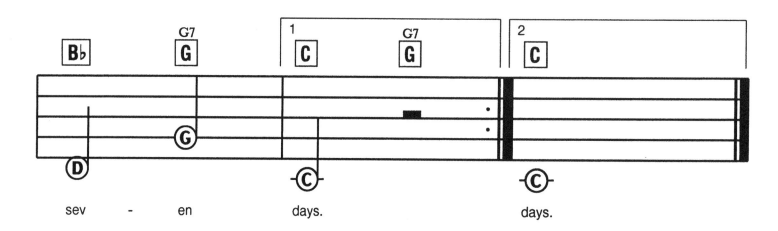

days, sev - en days, the week has

sev - en days. days.

Happy Birthday, Happy Birthday

Registration 2
Rhythm: Waltz

Words and Music by
Fred Rogers

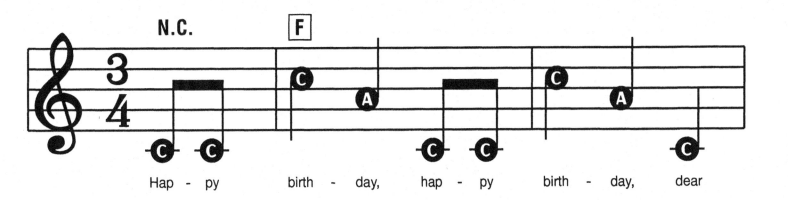

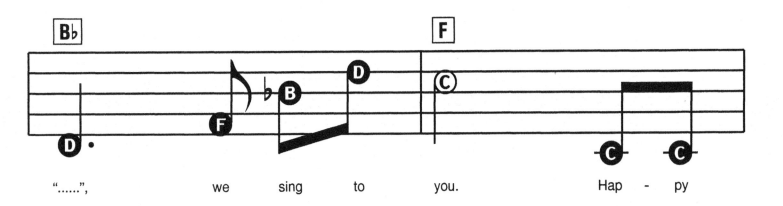

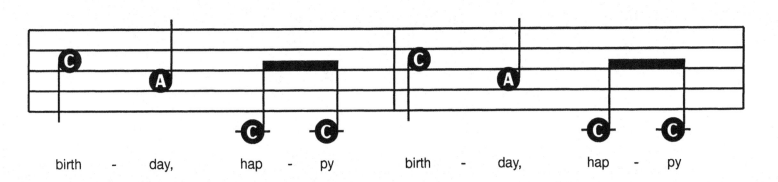

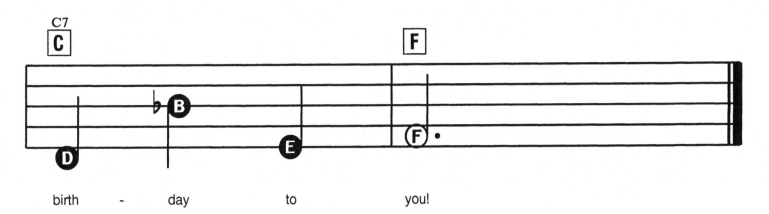

Everything Grows Together

Registration 1
Rhythm: 8-Beat or Pops

Words and Music by
Fred Rogers

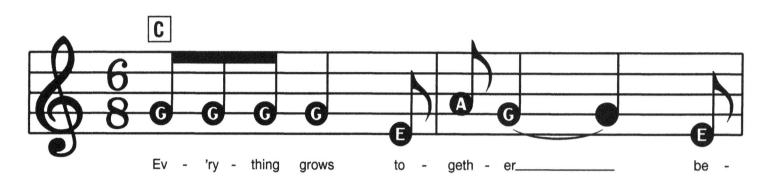

Ev - 'ry - thing grows to - geth - er_____ be -

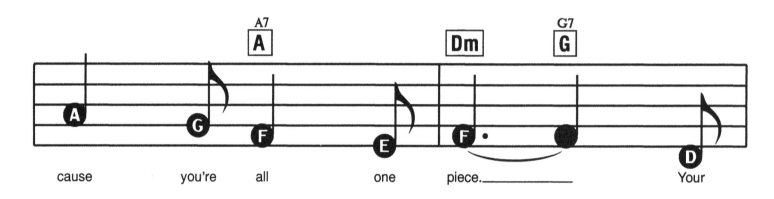

cause you're all one piece._____ Your

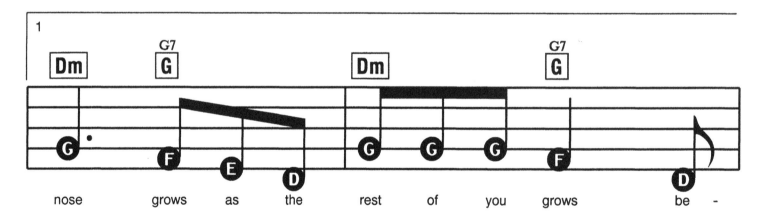

nose grows as the rest of you grows be -

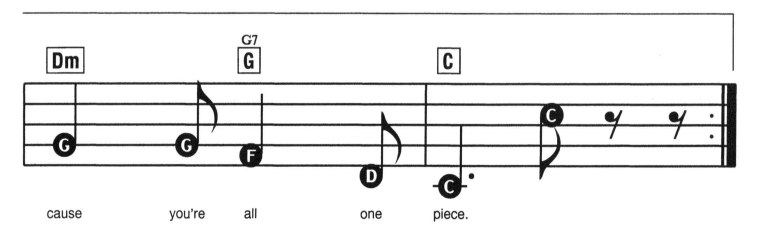

cause you're all one piece.

2-8

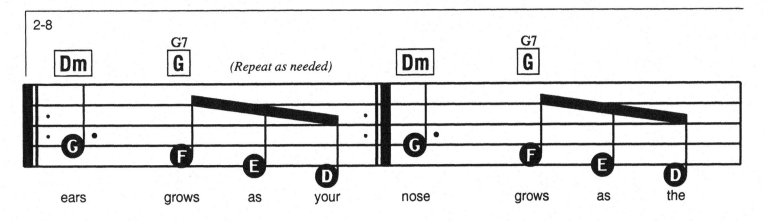

ears   grows   as   your   nose   grows   as   the

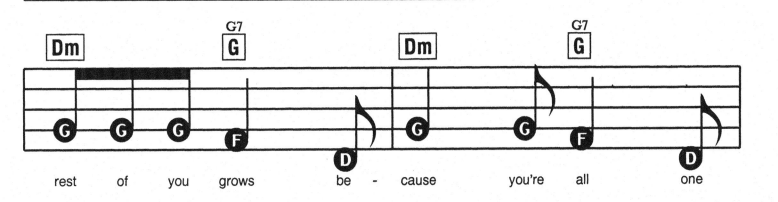

rest   of   you   grows   be - cause   you're   all   one

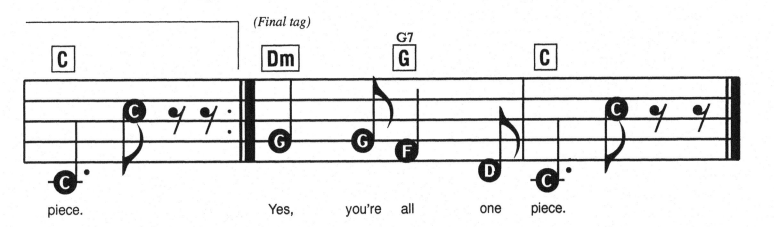

piece.   Yes,   you're   all   one   piece.

Additional body parts
(add cumulatively)

1. (nose)
2. (ears)
3. arms
4. hands
5. fingers
6. legs
7. feet
8. toes

Going to Marry Mom

Registration 9
Rhythm: Shuffle or Swing

Words and Music by
Fred Rogers

N.C. **F** **C7** **C** **F** **Dm**

C F E F G A A G G F A

One   day   I   said,   "I'm   real - ly   going   to   mar - ry,
2.-8. *(See additional lyrics)*

Gm **C7** **C** **F**

G G F F E G A A G G F A C

real - ly   going   to   mar - ry,   real - ly   going   to   mar - ry,"   I

C7 **C** **F** **Dm**

F E F G A A G G F A

told   my   mom,   "I'm   real - ly   going   to   mar - ry,

Gm **C7** **C** **1-7 F**

B♭ B♭ A A G C F C

real - ly   going   to   mar - ry   you."   She

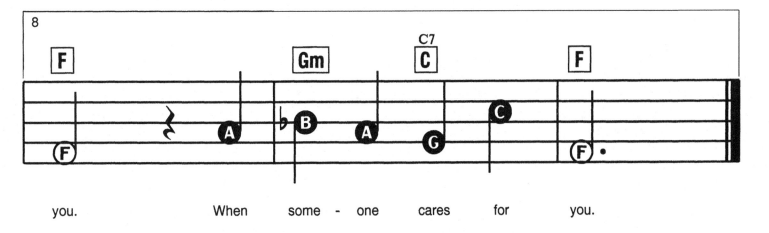

you. When some - one cares for you.

Additional Lyrics

2. She smiled, didn't laugh, said,
   "I hope you will marry, I hope you will marry,
   I hope you will marry."
   She smiled, didn't laugh, said,
   "I hope you will marry,
   maybe someone like me."

3. "But you see," she said, "I'm *(already married)**...
   I'm married to your daddy."

4. And as you grow more and *(more like your daddy)**...
   you'll find a person like me.

5. And she'll love you as *(I love your daddy)**...
   and she will marry you.

6. That's what Mom said when I *(told her I would marry)**...her.

7. I'm glad I told her 'cause I *(really often wondered)**...
   who my wife would be.

8. It all works out if you *(talk and you listen)**...
   when someone cares for you.

* *Repeat as needed*

I Like to Be Told

Registration 3
Rhythm: Slow Rock or Shuffle

Words and Music by
Fred Rogers

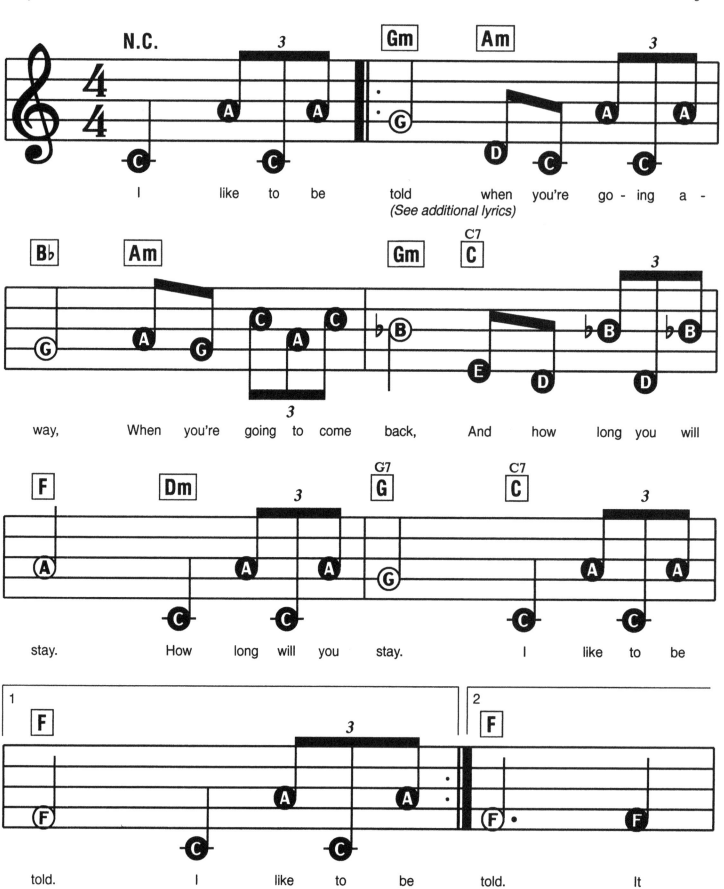

(See additional lyrics)

11

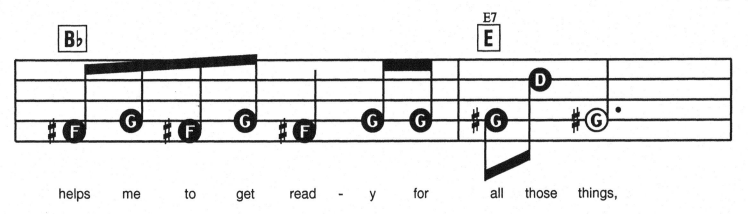

helps me to get read - y for all those things,

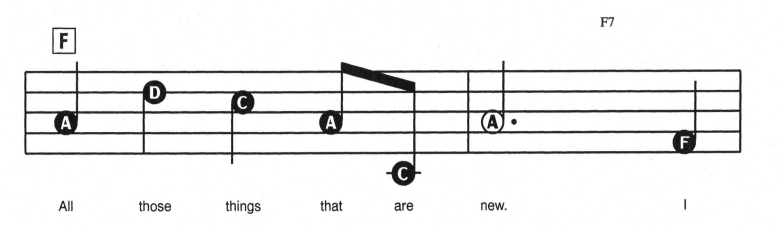

All those things that are new. I

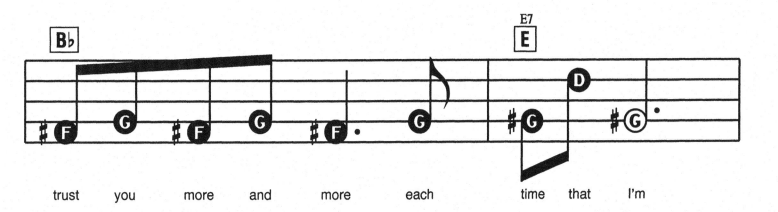

trust you more and more each time that I'm

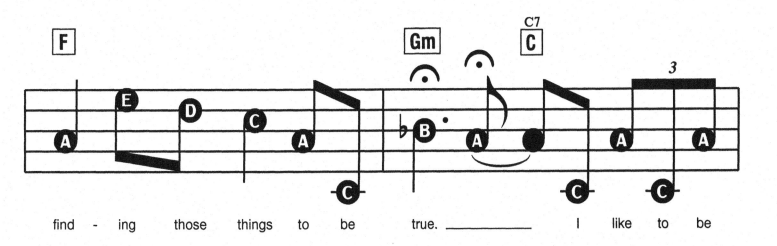

find - ing those things to be true. _____ I like to be

12

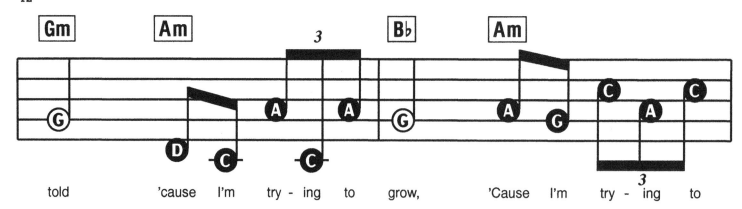

told   'cause I'm try - ing to grow,   'Cause I'm try - ing to

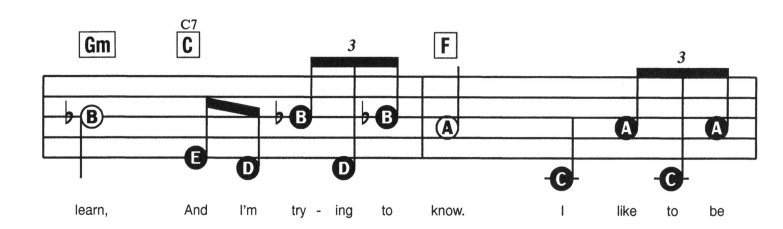

learn,   And I'm try - ing to know.   I like to be

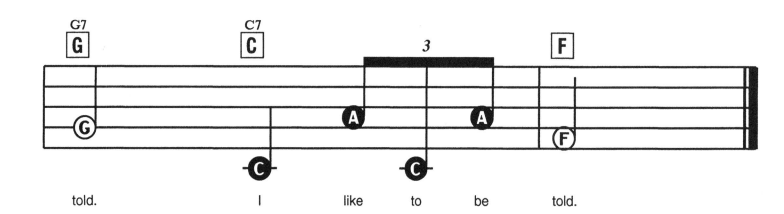

told.   I like to be told.

Additional Lyrics

I like to be told
If it's going to hurt,
If it's going to be hard,
If it's not going to hurt,
I like to be told.
I like to be told.

I'm Taking Care of You

Registration 8
Rhythm: March or Waltz

Words and Music by
Fred Rogers

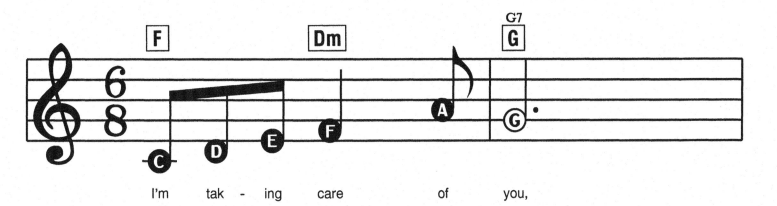

I'm tak - ing care of you,

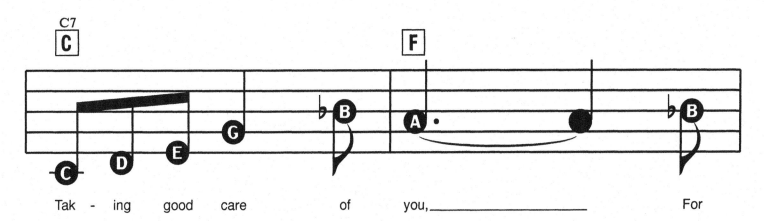

Tak - ing good care of you,_____ For

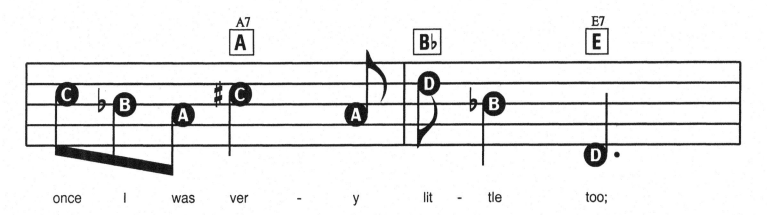

once I was ver - y lit - tle too;

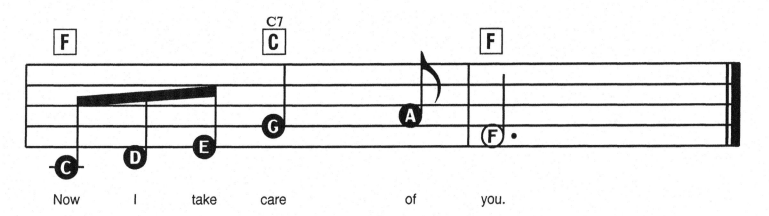

Now I take care of you.

It's Such a Good Feeling

Registration 4
Rhythm: Samba or March

Words and Music by
Fred Rogers

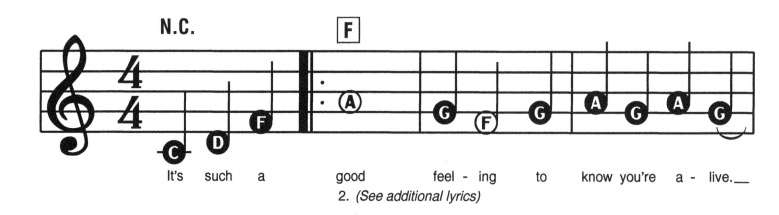

It's such a good feel - ing to know you're a - live.__
2. *(See additional lyrics)*

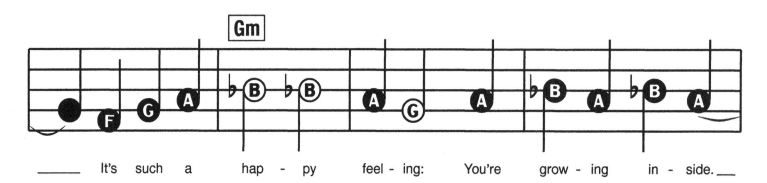

___ It's such a hap - py feel - ing: You're grow - ing in - side.__

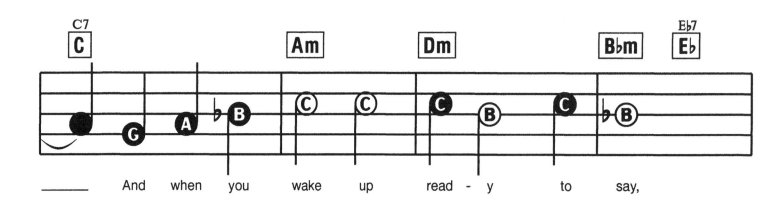

___ And when you wake up read - y to say,

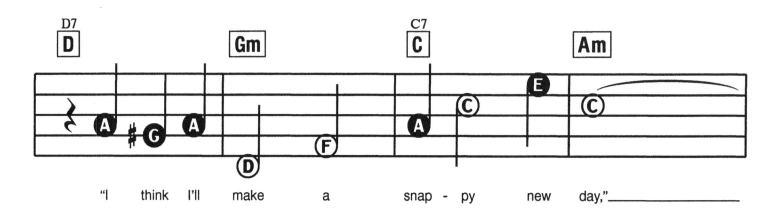

"I think I'll make a snap - py new day,"_____

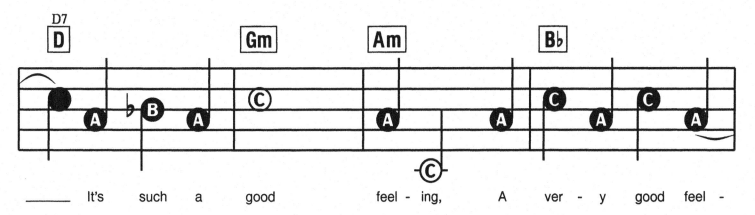

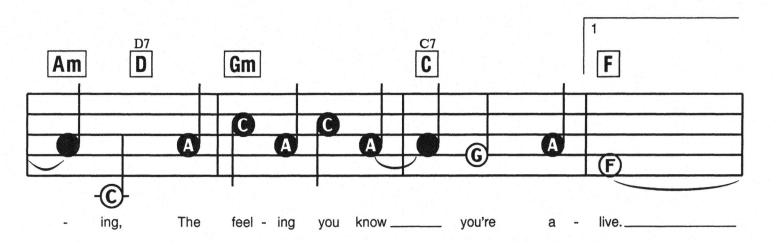

It's such a good feel - ing, A ver - y good feel -

- ing, The feel - ing you know _____ you're a - live. _____

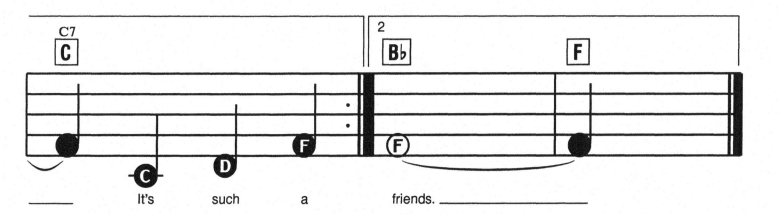

_____ It's such a friends. _____

Additional Lyrics

It's such a good feeling
to know you're in tune.
It's such a happy feeling
to find you're in bloom.
And when you wake up ready to say,
"I think I'll make a snappy new day,"
It's such a good feeling,
A very good feeling,
The feeling you know that we're friends.

Just for Once

Registration 1
Rhythm: 8-Beat or Pops

Words and Music by
Fred Rogers

(See additional lyrics)

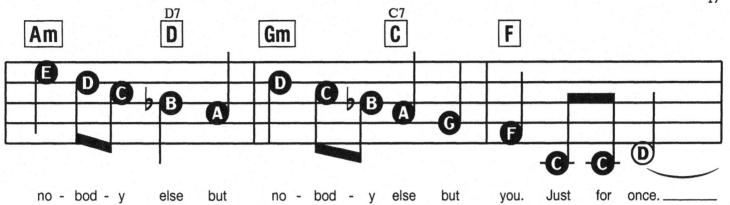

no - bod - y else but no - bod - y else but you. Just for once. _____

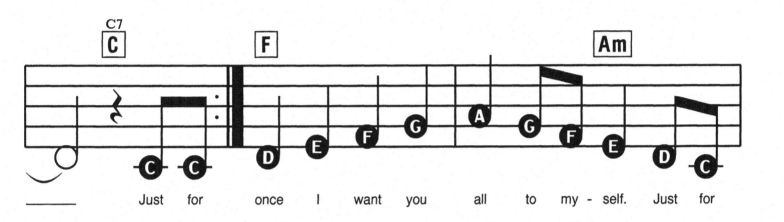

_____ Just for once I want you all to my - self. Just for

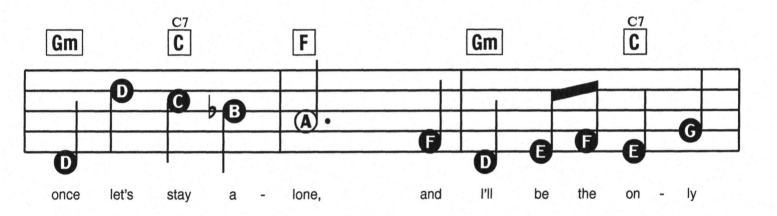

once let's stay a - lone, and I'll be the on - ly

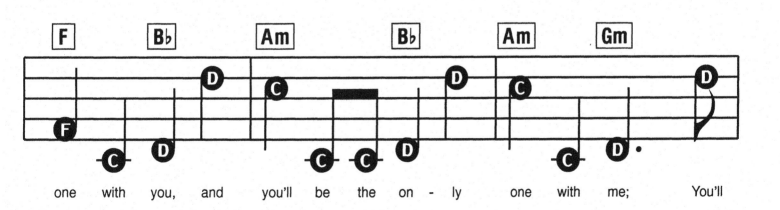

one with you, and you'll be the on - ly one with me; You'll

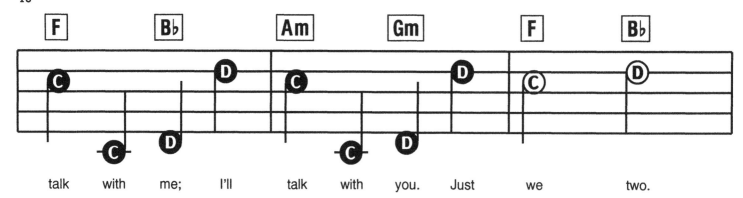

talk   with   me;   I'll   talk   with   you.   Just   we   two.

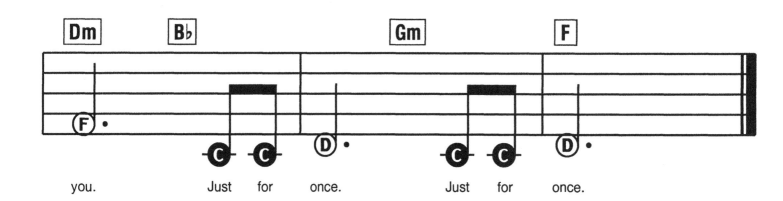

No - bod - y   else,   but   no - bod - y   else   but

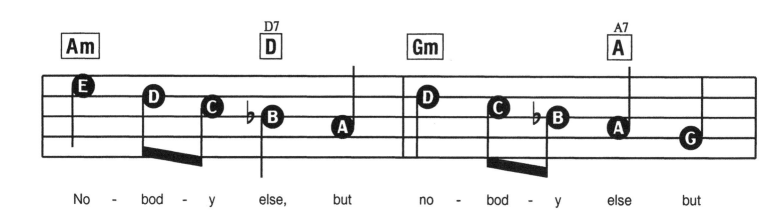

you.   Just   for   once.   Just   for   once.

Additional Lyrics

Just for once,
I want you all to myself.
Just for once let's play alone
With nobody else.
We'll build us
A house with...a garden—
And no, no, nobody else but
Nobody else but you
Just for once.

One and One Are Two

Registration 1
Rhythm: Pops or Rock

Words and Music by
Fred Rogers

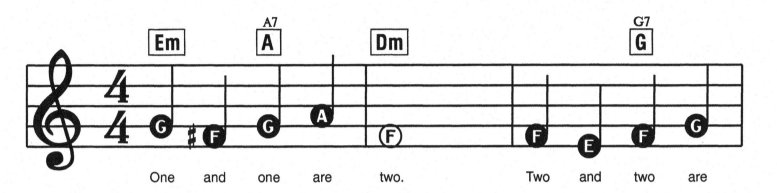

One and one are two. Two and two are

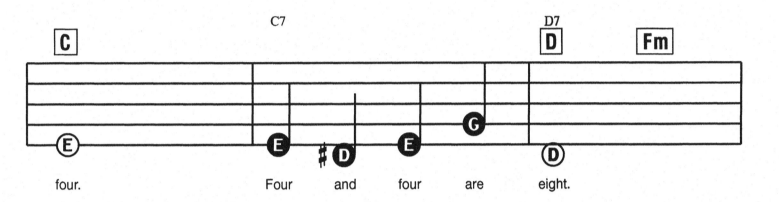

four. Four and four are eight.

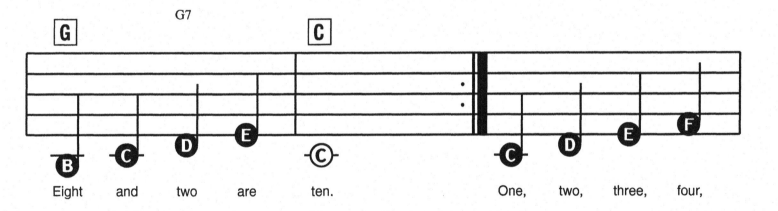

Eight and two are ten. One, two, three, four,

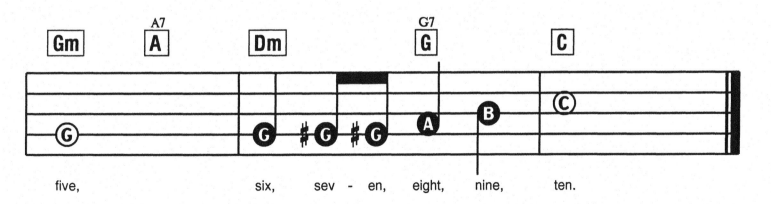

five, six, sev - en, eight, nine, ten.

Let's Think of Something to Do
(While We're Waiting)

Registration 7
Rhythm: March

Words and Music by
Fred Rogers

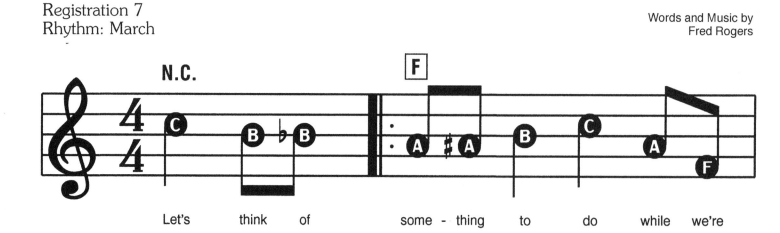

Let's think of some - thing to do while we're

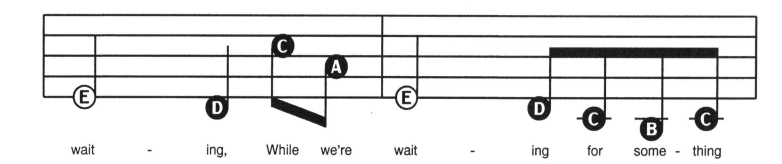

wait - ing, While we're wait - ing for some - thing

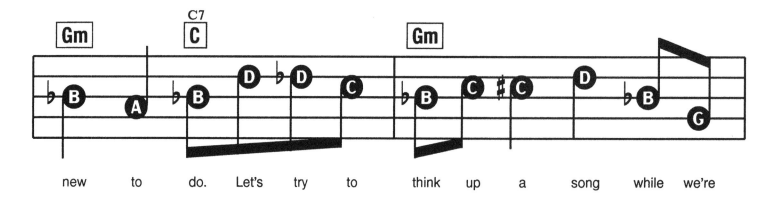

new to do. Let's try to think up a song while we're

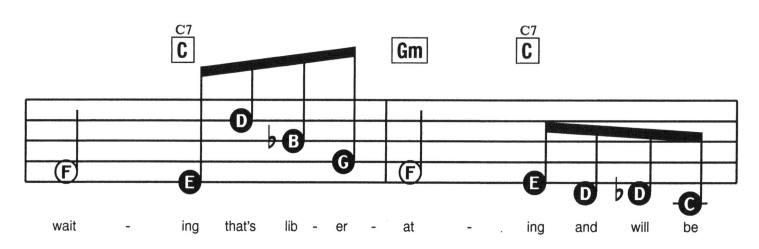

wait - ing that's lib - er - at - ing and will be

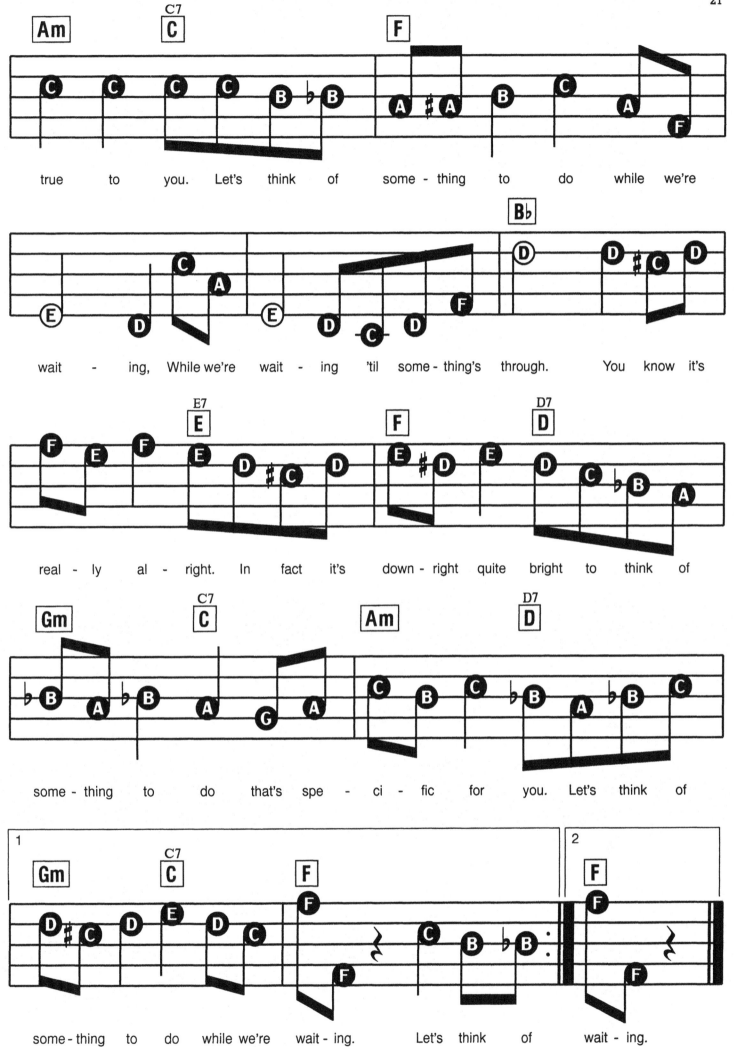

Please Don't Think It's Funny

Registration 3
Rhythm: Waltz

Words and Music by
Fred Rogers

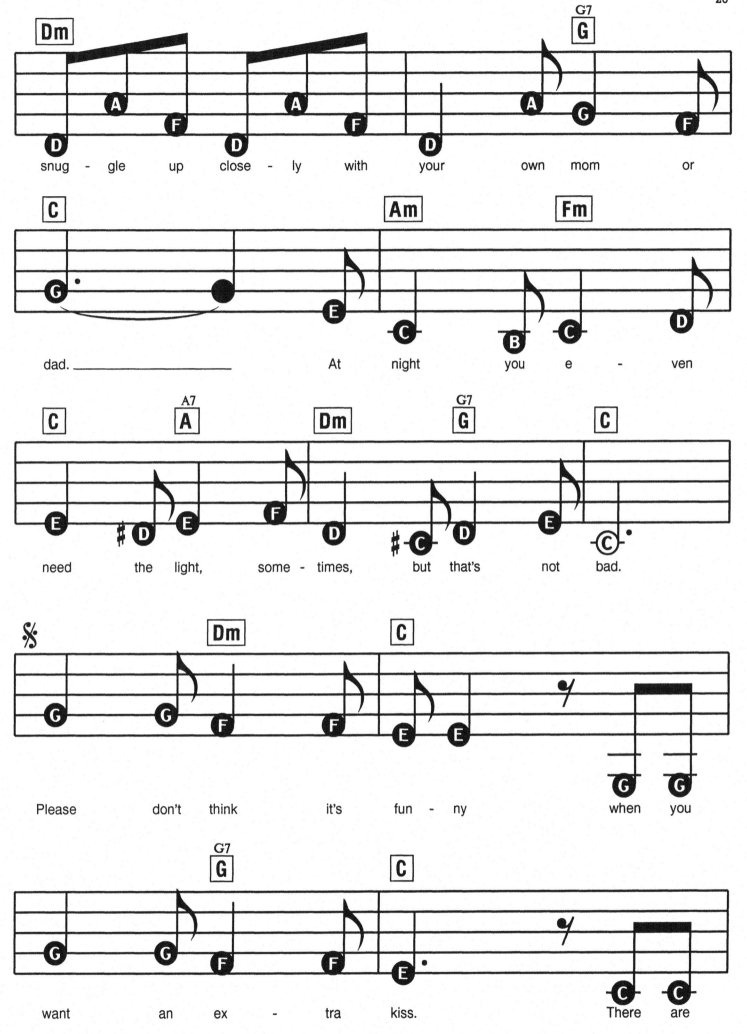

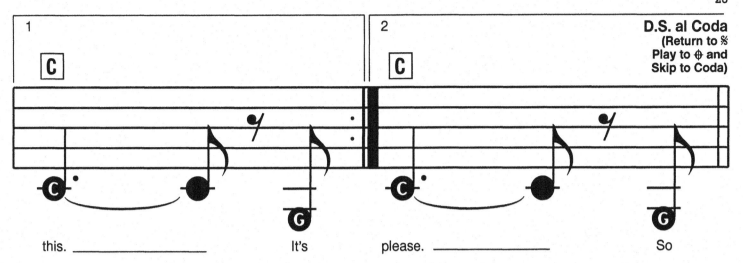

D.S. al Coda
(Return to ⅹ
Play to ⊕ and
Skip to Coda)

CODA

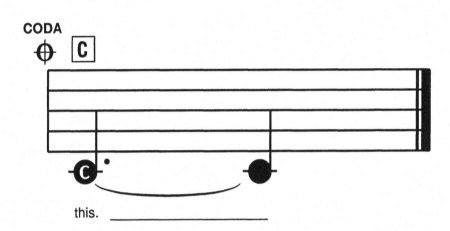

Additional Lyrics

2. It's great to know you're growing up bigger every day.
   But somehow things you like to remember
   Are often put away.
   And sometimes you wonder over and over
   If you should stay inside.
   When you enjoy a younger toy...
   You never need to hide.

   In the long trip of growing
   There are stops along the way
   For thoughts of all the soft things
   And a look at yesterday.
   For a chance to fill our feelings,
   With comfort and with ease,
   And then tell the new tomorrow,
   "You can come now when you please."

(D.S.) So please don't think it's funny, when you want an extra kiss.
   There are lots and lots of people who sometimes feel like this.

   Please don't think it's funny when you want the ones you miss.
   There are lots and lots of people who sometimes feel like this.

There Are Many Ways
(To Say I Love You)

Registration 2
Rhythm: 8-Beat or Pops

Words and Music by
Fred Rogers

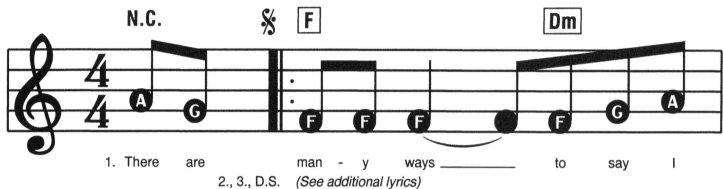

1. There are man-y ways _____ to say I
2., 3., D.S. *(See additional lyrics)*

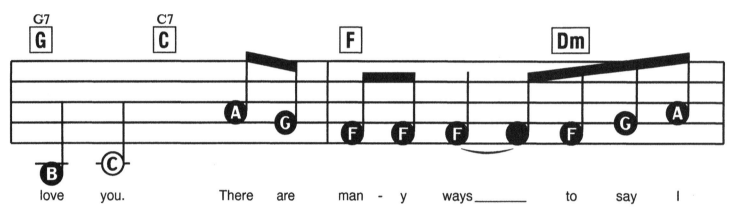

love you. There are man-y ways _____ to say I

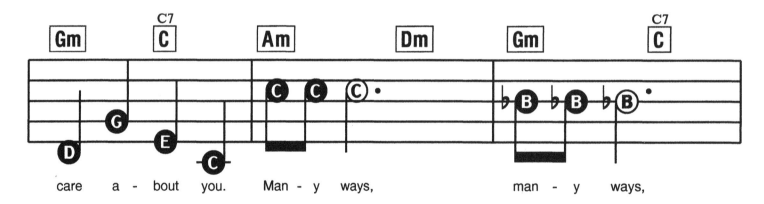

care a-bout you. Man-y ways, man-y ways,

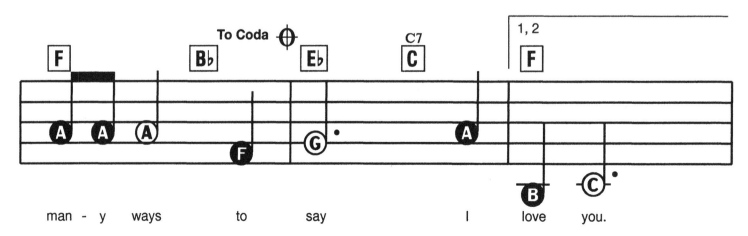

man-y ways to say I love you.

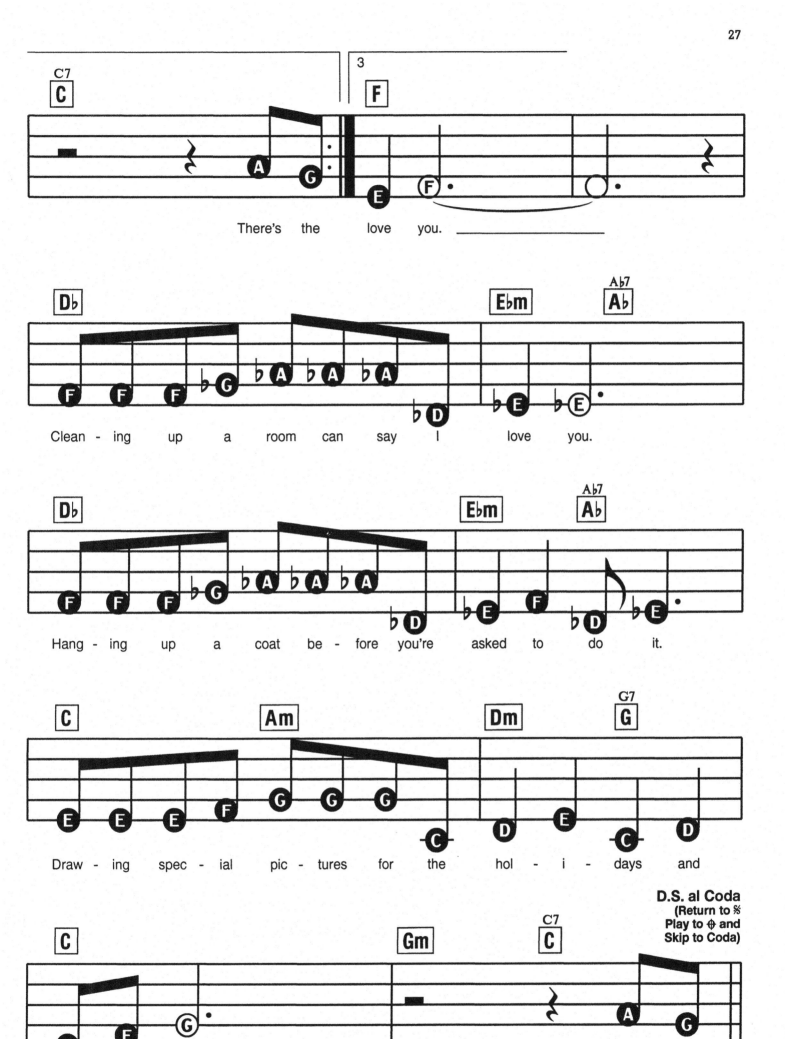

There's the love you. _____

Clean - ing up a room can say I love you.

Hang - ing up a coat be - fore you're asked to do it.

Draw - ing spec - ial pic - tures for the hol - i - days and

D.S. al Coda
(Return to ℅
Play to ⊕ and
Skip to Coda)

mak - ing plays.

There are

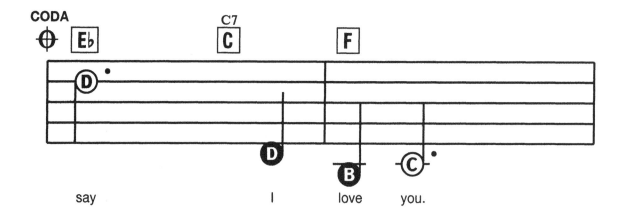

say   I   love   you.

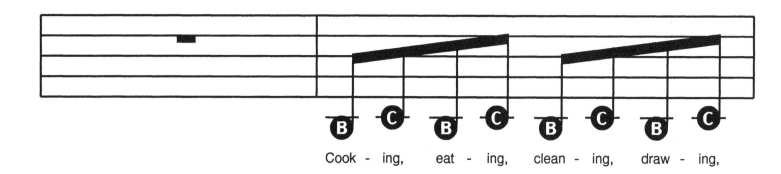

Cook - ing,   eat - ing,   clean - ing,   draw - ing,

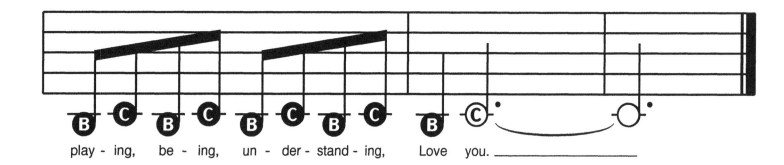

play - ing, be - ing, un - der - stand - ing,   Love   you. _____

Additional Lyrics

2. There's the cooking way to say I love you.
   There's the cooking something
   someone really likes to eat.
   The cooking way, the cooking way,
   the cooking way to say
   I love you.

3. There's the eating way to say I love you.
   There's the eating something
   someone made especially.
   The eating way, the eating way,
   the eating way to say
   I love you.

(D.S.) There are many ways to say I love you.
   Just by being there when things are
   sad and scary.
   Just by being there, being there,
   being there to say
   I love you.

Peace and Quiet

Registration 10
Rhythm: 8-Beat or Pops

Words and Music by
Fred Rogers

Sometimes

Registration 2
Rhythm: 8-Beat or Rock

Words and Music by
Fred Rogers

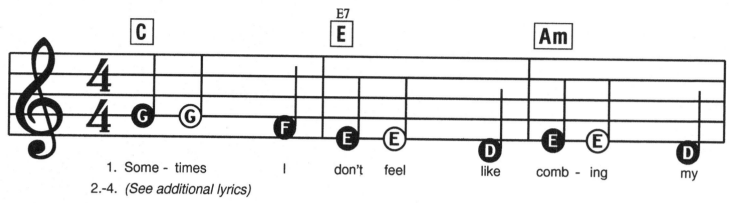

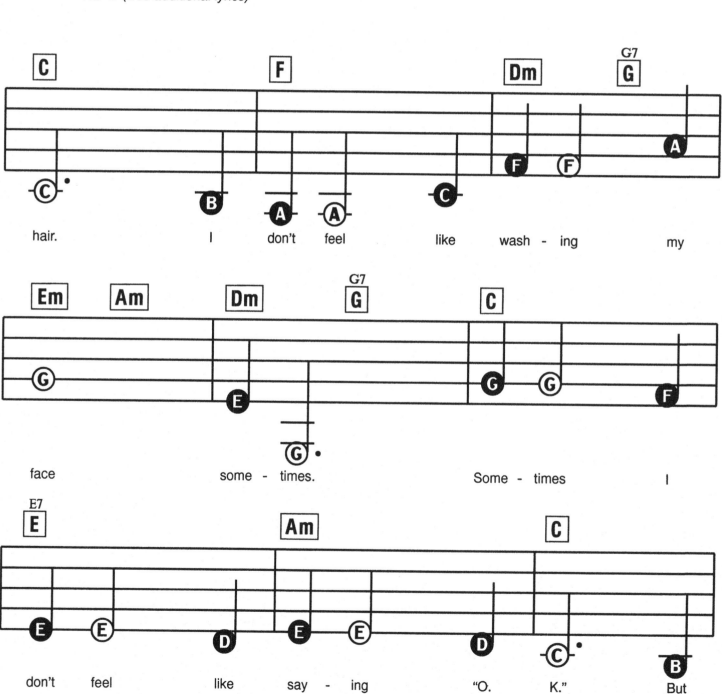

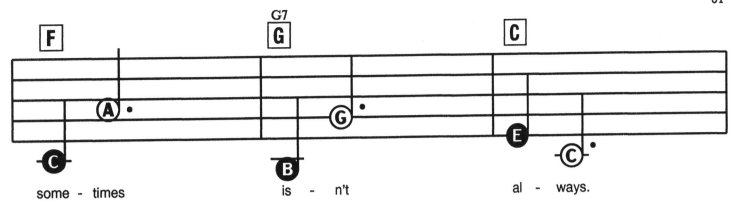

some - times   is - n't   al - ways.

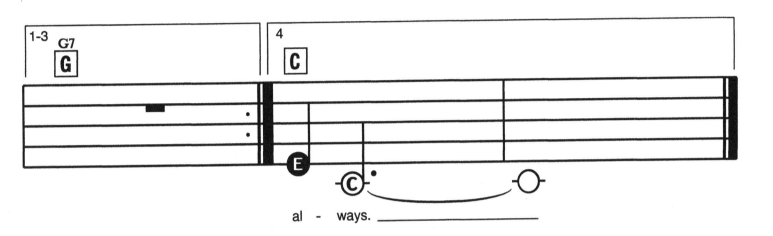

al - ways. _____

Additional Lyrics

2. Sometimes I do feel like combing my hair.
   I do feel like washing my face sometimes.
   Sometimes I do feel like saying "O.K."
   But sometimes isn't always.

3. Sometimes I don't feel like going to bed.
   I don't feel like getting right up sometimes.
   Sometimes I don't feel like wearing my shoes.
   But sometimes isn't always.

4. Sometimes I don't feel like sometimes I do.
   I feel like I don't like to feel sometimes.
   Sometimes I don't and sometimes I do.
   But sometimes isn't always.

Sometimes People Are Good

Registration 8
Rhythm: 8-Beat or Rock

Words and Music by
Fred Rogers

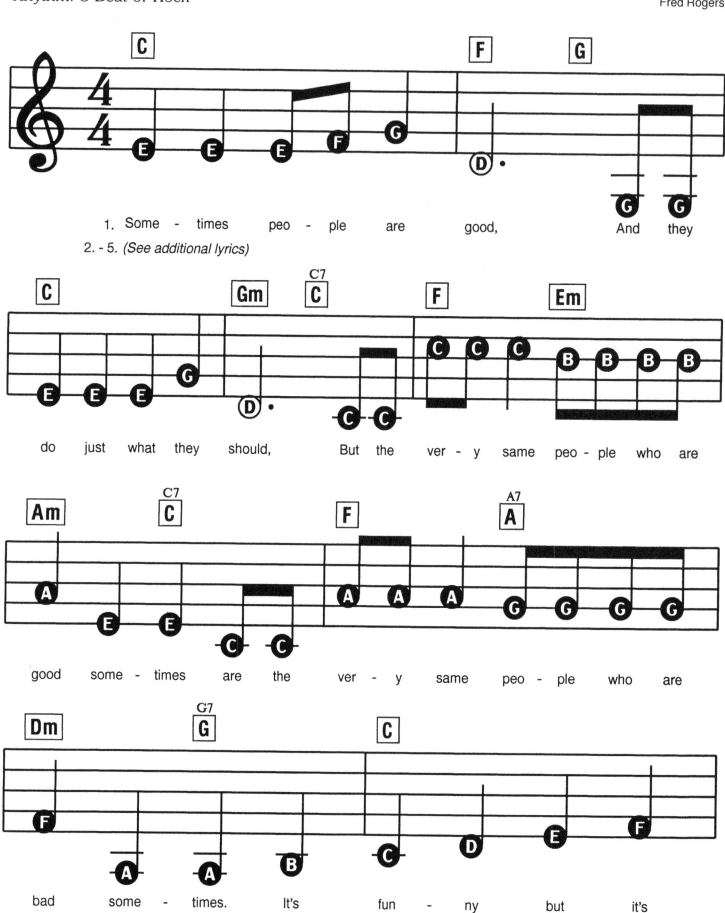

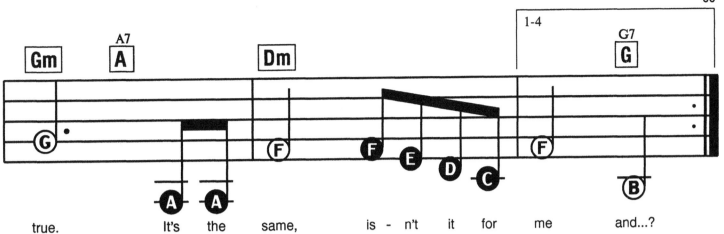

true.   It's the same,   is - n't it for me and...?

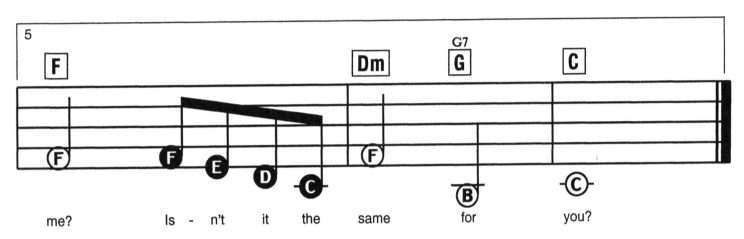

me?   Is - n't it the same for you?

Additional Lyrics

2. Sometimes people get wet.
   And their parents get upset.
   But the very same people who are wet sometimes
   Are the very same people who are dry sometimes.
   It's funny but it's true.
   It's the same, isn't it for
   Me and...

3. Sometimes people make noise,
   And they break each other's toys.
   But the very same people who are noisy sometimes
   Are the very same people who are quiet sometimes.
   It's funny but it's true.
   It's the same, isn't it for
   Me and...

4. Sometimes people get mad,
   And they feel like being bad.
   But the very same people who are mad sometimes
   Are the very same people who are glad sometimes.
   It's funny but it's true.
   It's the same, isn't it for
   Me and...

5. Sometimes people are good,
   And they do just what they should.
   But the very same people who are good sometimes
   Are the very same people who are bad sometimes.
   It's funny but it's true.
   It's the same, isn't it for
   Me...Isn't it the same for you?

Then Your Heart Is Full of Love

Registration 5
Rhythm: Rock or Pops

Words by Josie Carey
Music by Fred Rogers

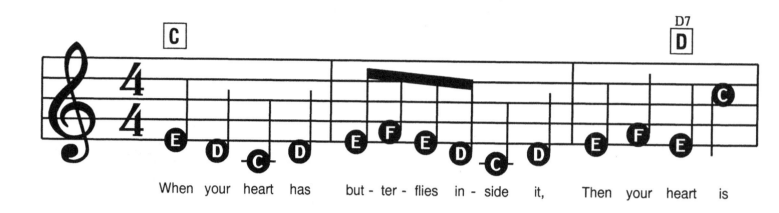

When your heart has but-ter-flies in-side it, Then your heart is

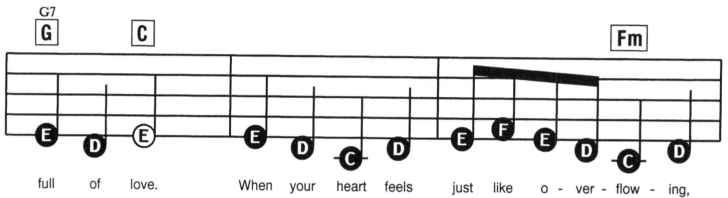

full of love. When your heart feels just like o-ver-flow-ing,

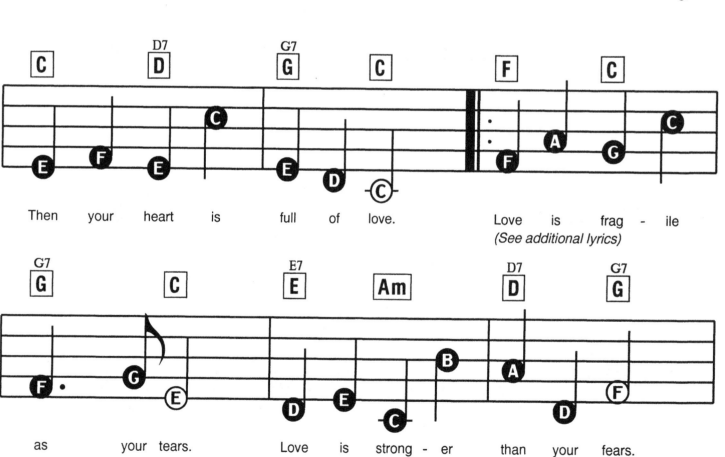

Then your heart is full of love. Love is frag-ile
(See additional lyrics)

as your tears. Love is strong-er than your fears.

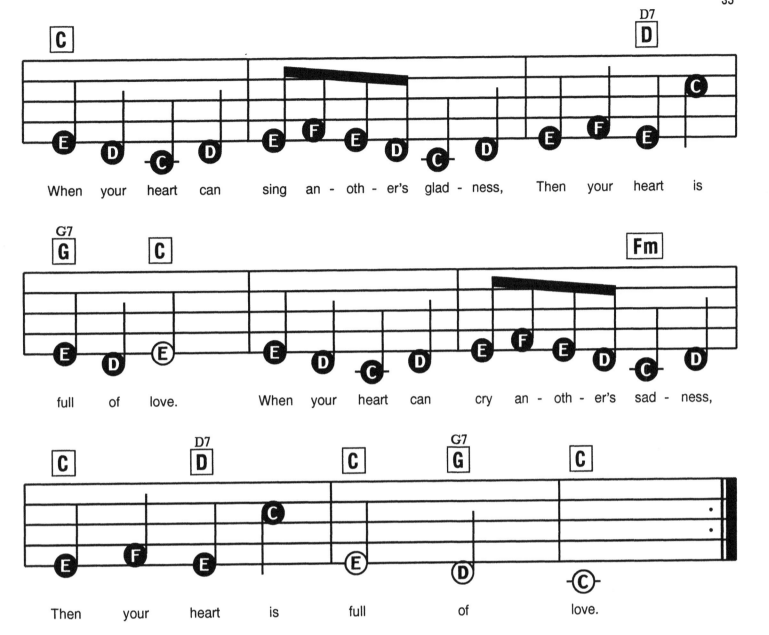

Additional Lyrics

Love is fragile as your tears.
Love is stronger than your fears.

When your heart beats for a special someone,
Then your heart is full of love.
When your heart has room for everybody,
Then your heart is full of love.

Tree, Tree, Tree

Registration 4
Rhythm: Waltz

Words and Music by
Fred Rogers

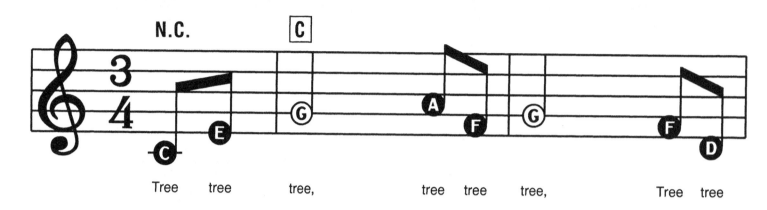

Tree tree tree, tree tree tree, Tree tree

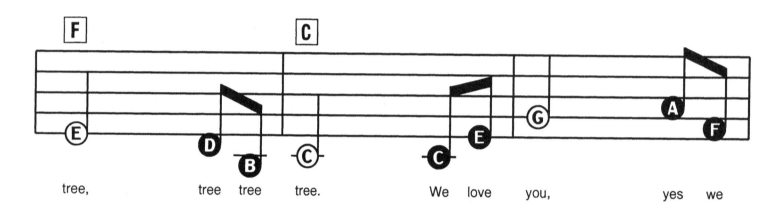

tree, tree tree tree. We love you, yes we

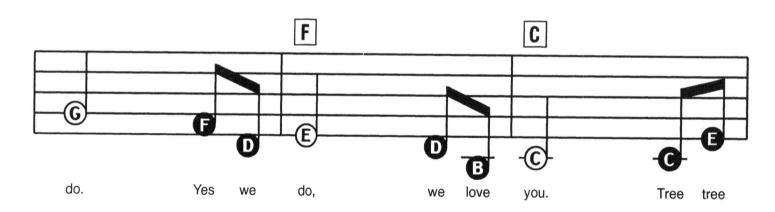

do. Yes we do, we love you. Tree tree

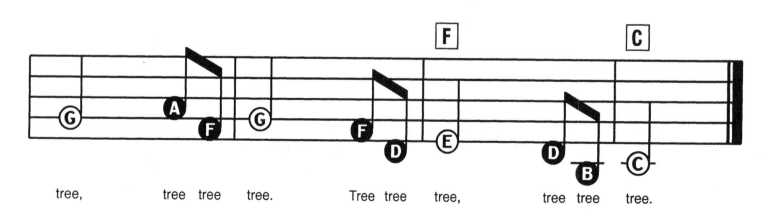

tree, tree tree tree. Tree tree tree, tree tree tree.

When the Day Turns Into Night

Registration 3
Rhythm: 8-Beat or Pops

Words and Music by
Fred Rogers

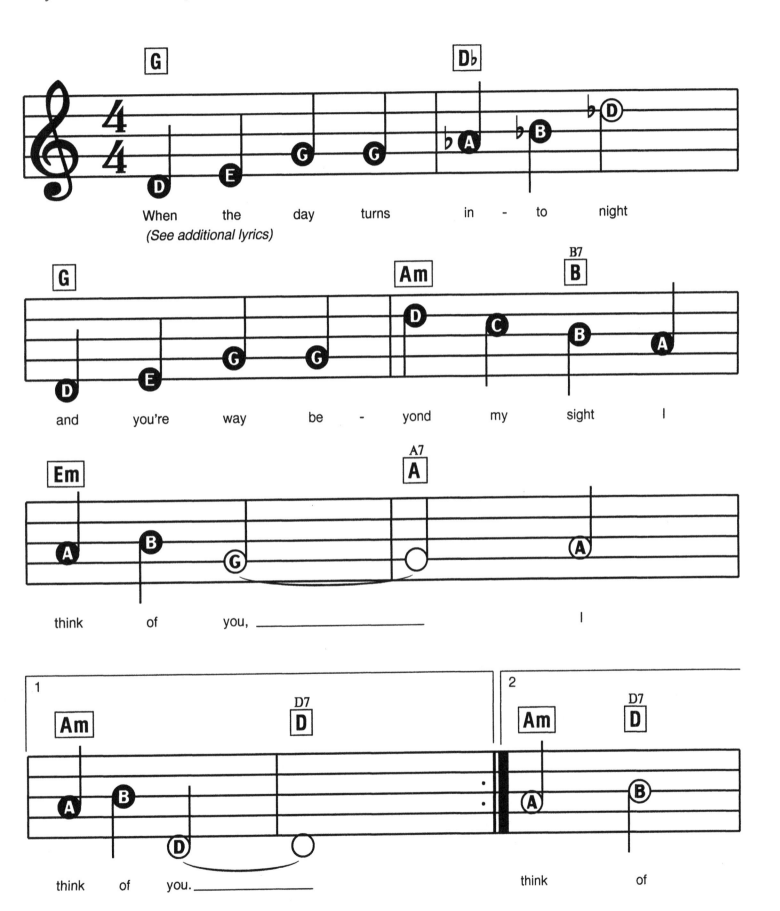

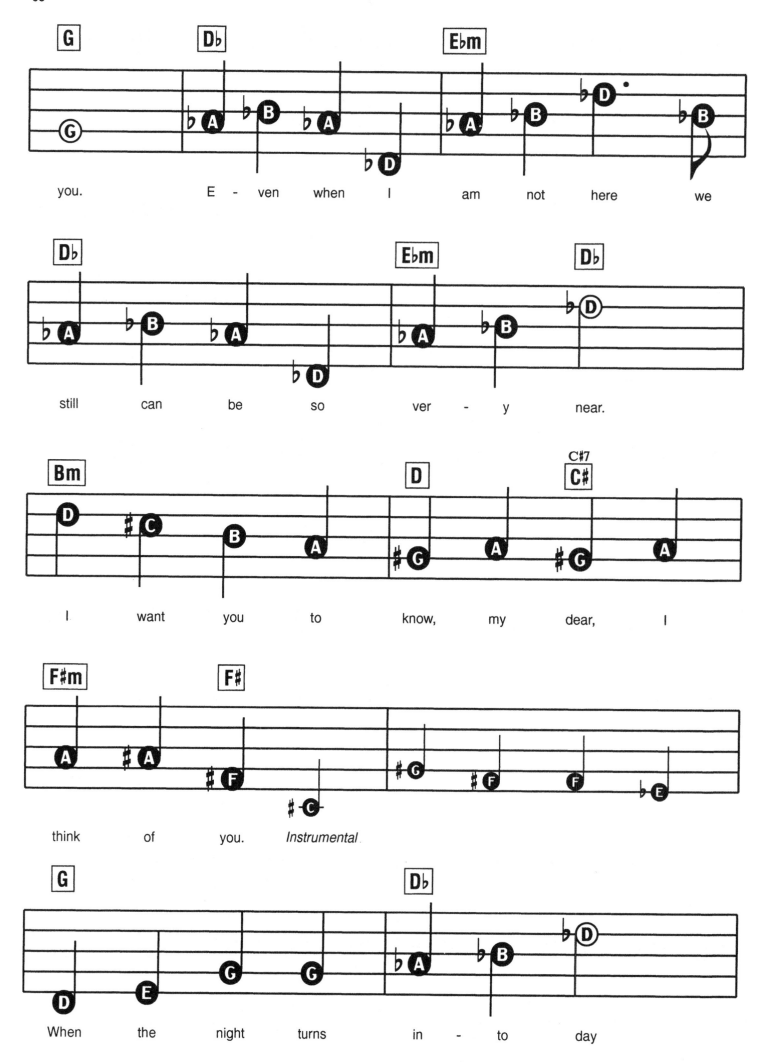

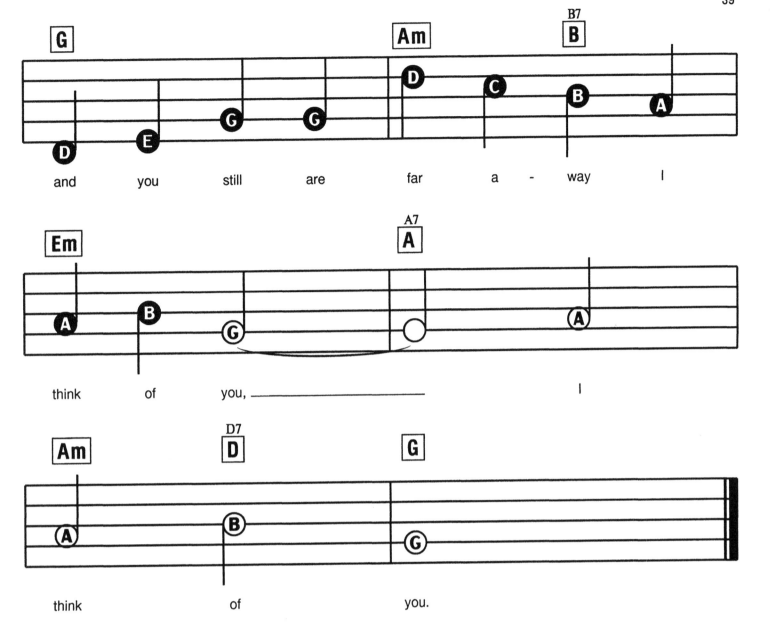

Additional Lyrics

When the night turns into day
And you still are far away
I think of you, I think of you.

What Do You Do?

Registration 7
Rhythm: Shuffle or Swing

Words and Music by
Fred Rogers

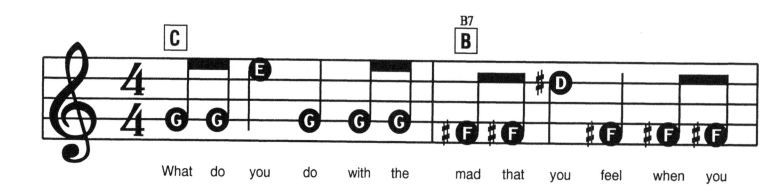

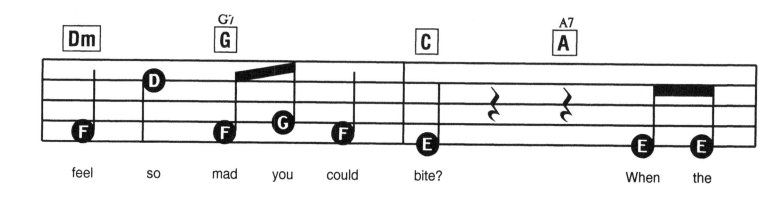

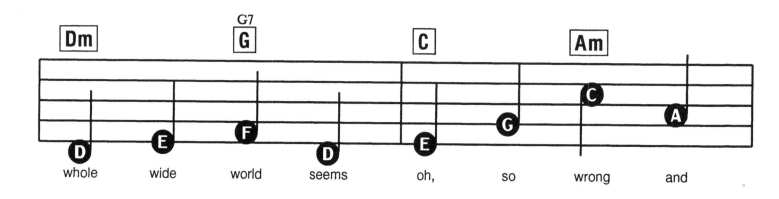

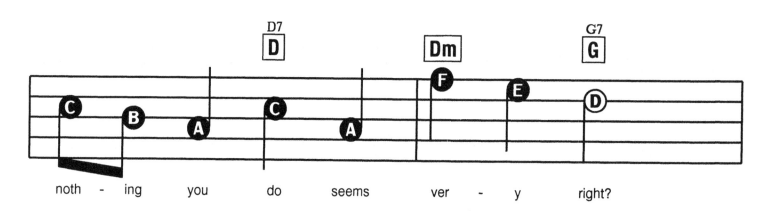

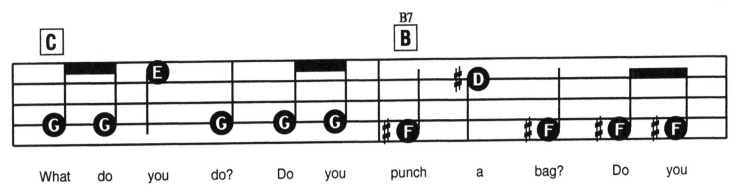

What do you do? Do you punch a bag? Do you

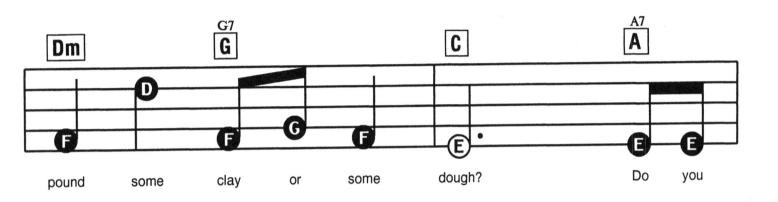

pound some clay or some dough? Do you

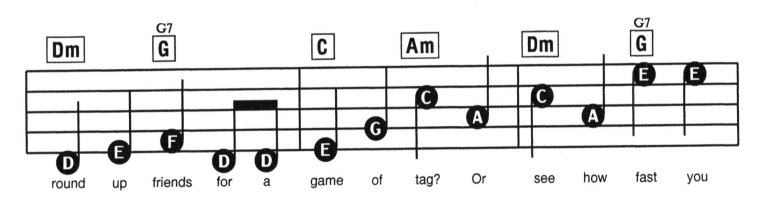

round up friends for a game of tag? Or see how fast you

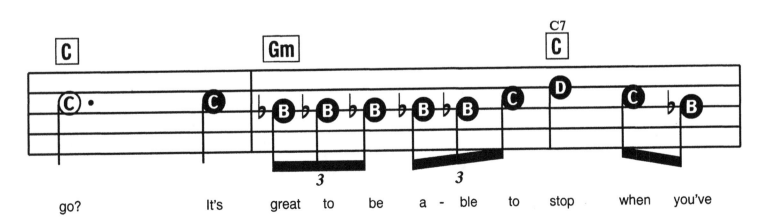

go? It's great to be a - ble to stop when you've

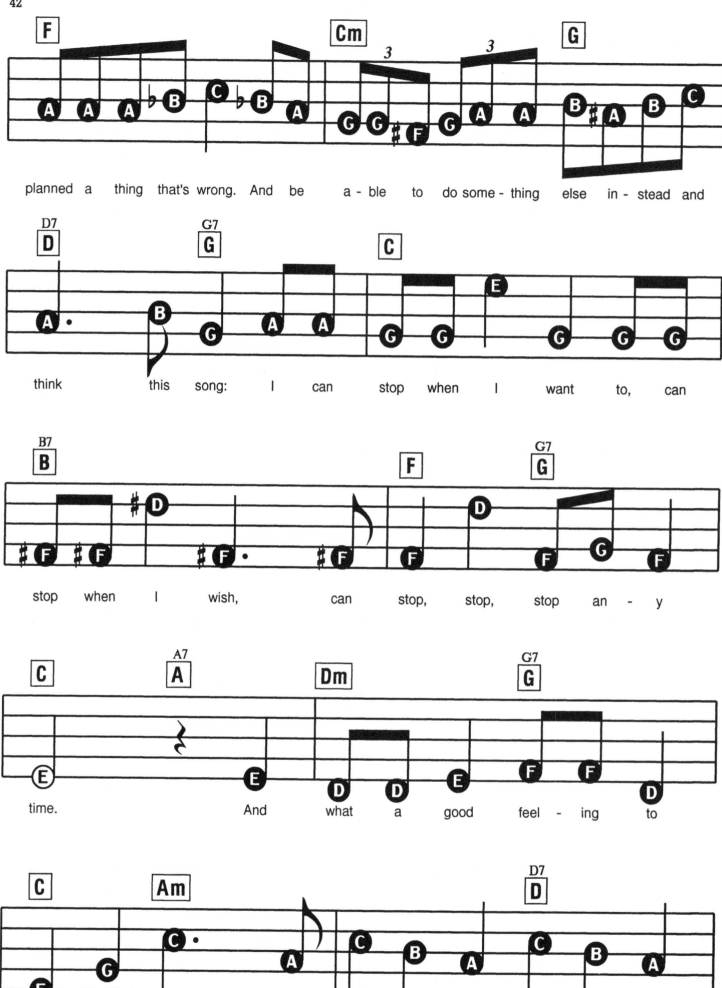

43

When a Baby Comes

Registration 3
Rhythm: 8-Beat or Pops

Words and Music by
Fred Rogers

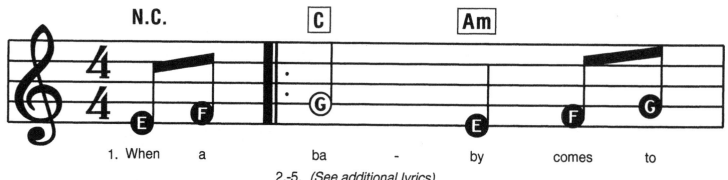

1. When a ba - by comes to

2.-5. *(See additional lyrics)*

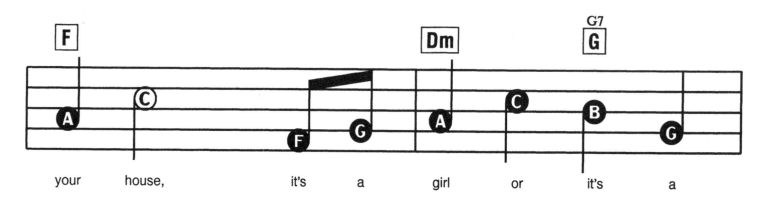

your house, it's a girl or it's a

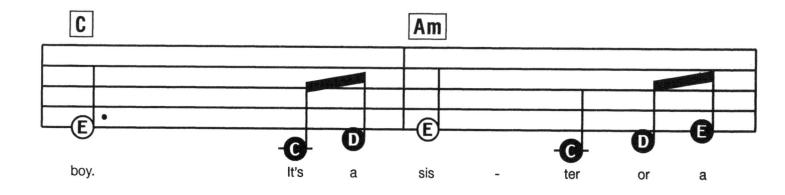

boy. It's a sis - ter or a

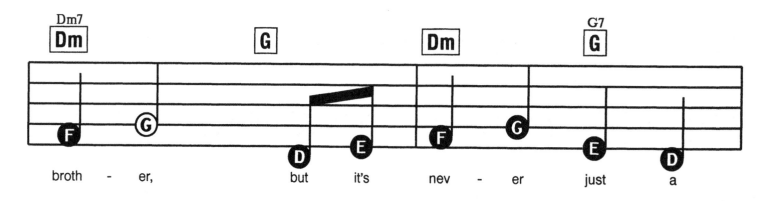

broth - er, but it's nev - er just a

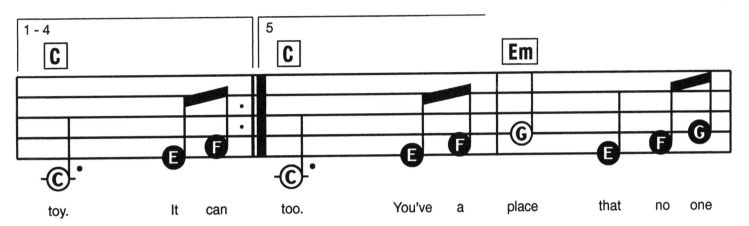

toy.   It   can   too.   You've   a   place   that   no   one

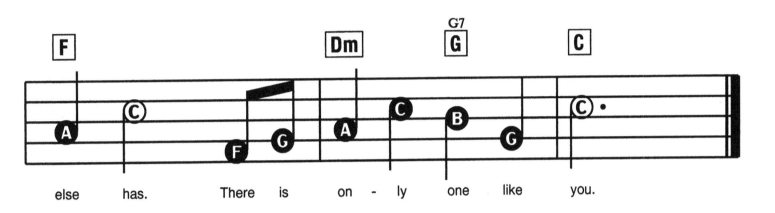

else   has.   There   is   on - ly   one   like   you.

Additional Lyrics

2. It can cry and it can holler
   It can wet and make a face
   But there's one thing it can never
   It can never take your place.

3. You were there before the baby
   Now the baby's always there.
   Now you wait for special moments
   With your mother in the chair.

4. You're a very special person
   You are special to your mom
   And your dad begins to say,
   "You'll always be the older one."

5. It's so good to know that always
   There's a special place for you
   And a special place for baby
   Right inside the family too.

   You've a place that no one else has.
   There is only one like you.

Won't You Be My Neighbor?
(It's a Beautiful Day in the Neighborhood)

Registration 8
Rhythm: Swing or Shuffle

Words and Music by
Fred Rogers

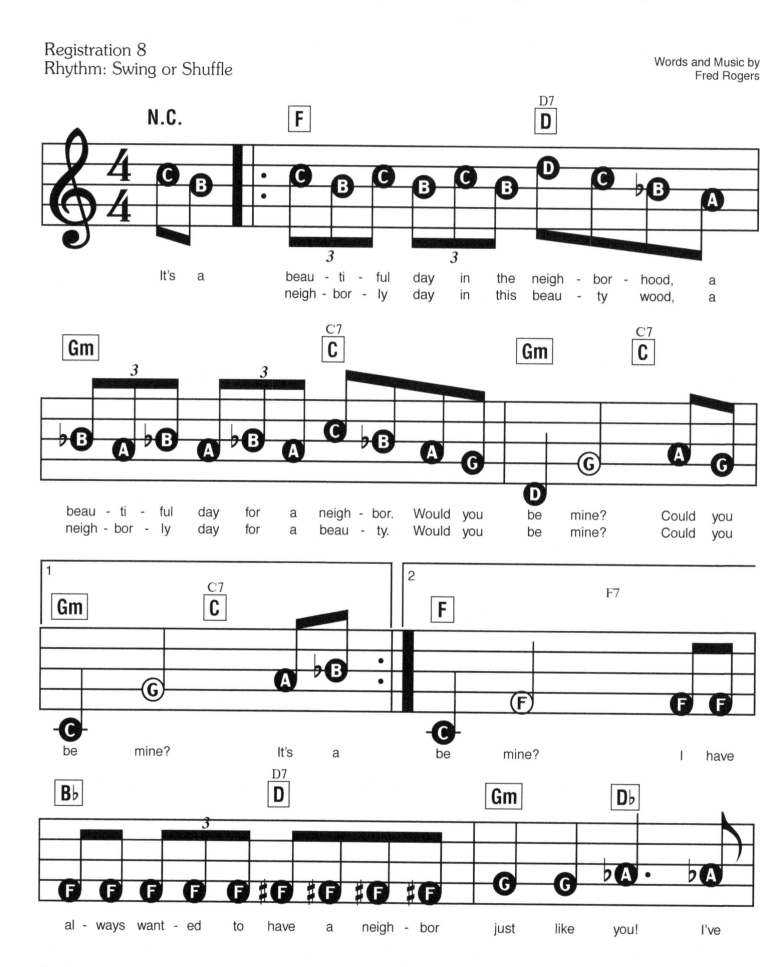

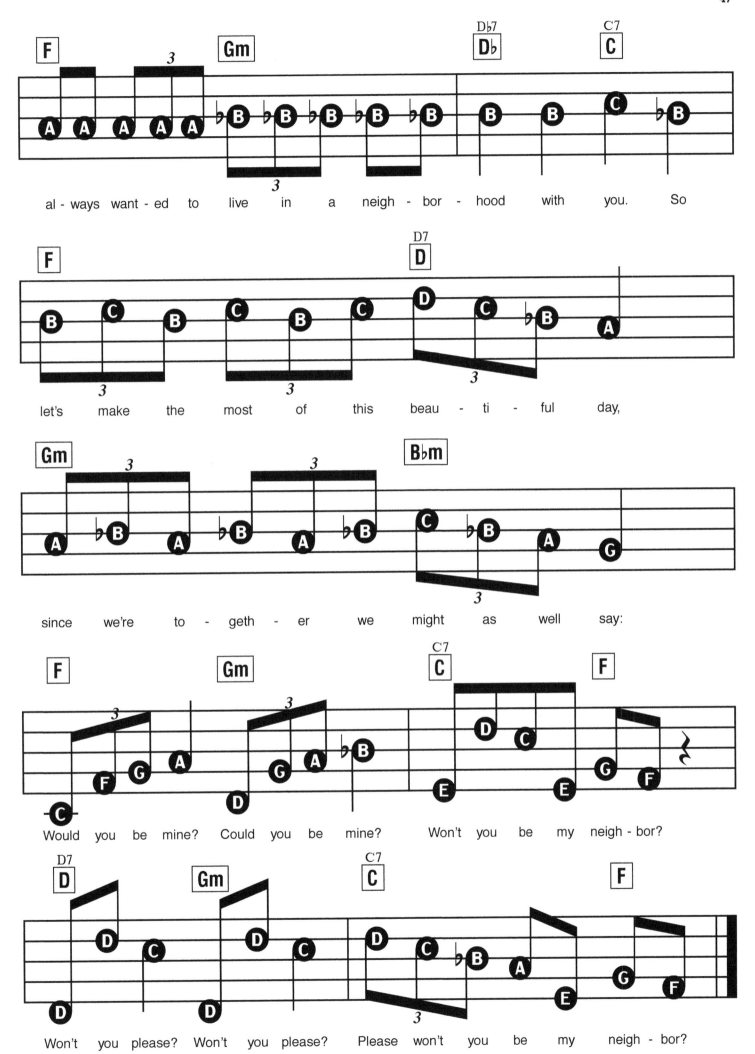

You Can Never
Go Down the Drain

Registration 4
Rhythm: 6/8 March

Words and Music by
Fred Rogers

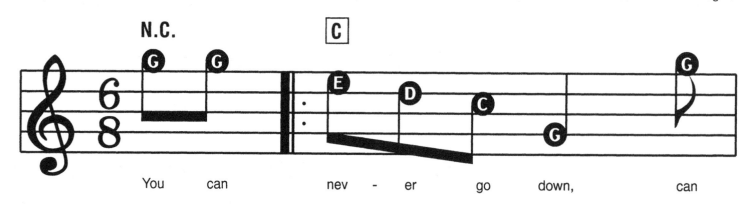

You   can   nev - er   go   down,   can

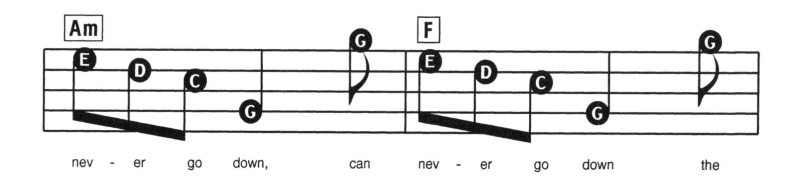

nev - er   go   down,   can   nev - er   go   down   the

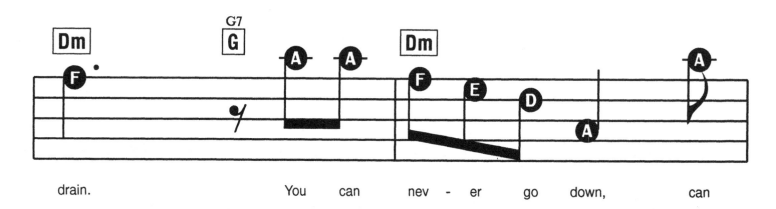

drain.   You   can   nev - er   go   down,   can

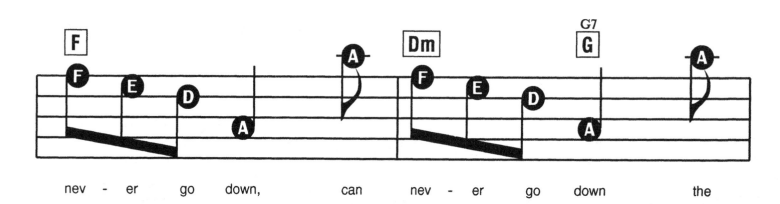

nev - er   go   down,   can   nev - er   go   down   the

1

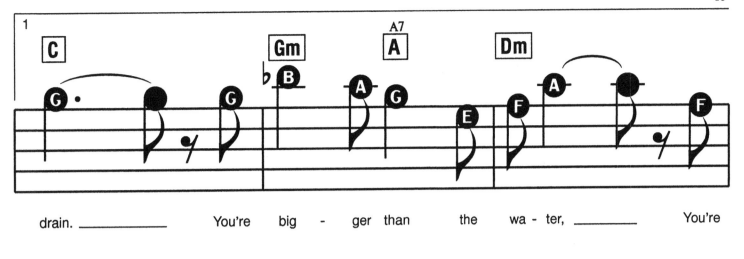

drain. _____ You're big - ger than the wa - ter, _____ You're

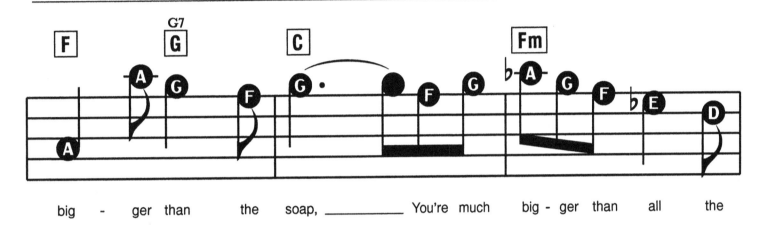

big - ger than the soap, _____ You're much big - ger than all the

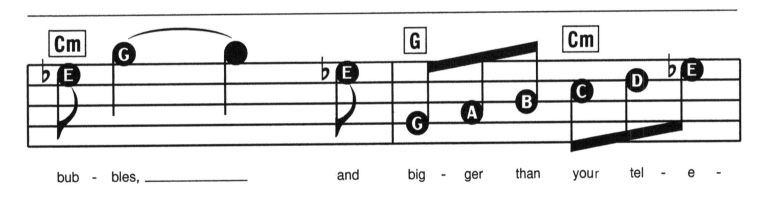

bub - bles, _____ and big - ger than your tel - e -

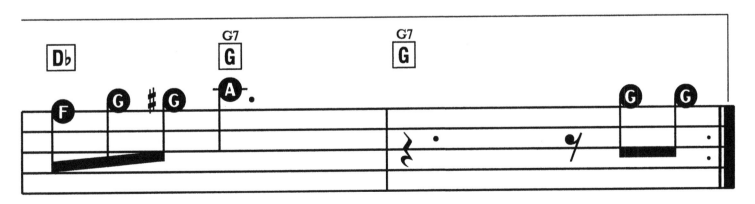

scope, so you see... You can

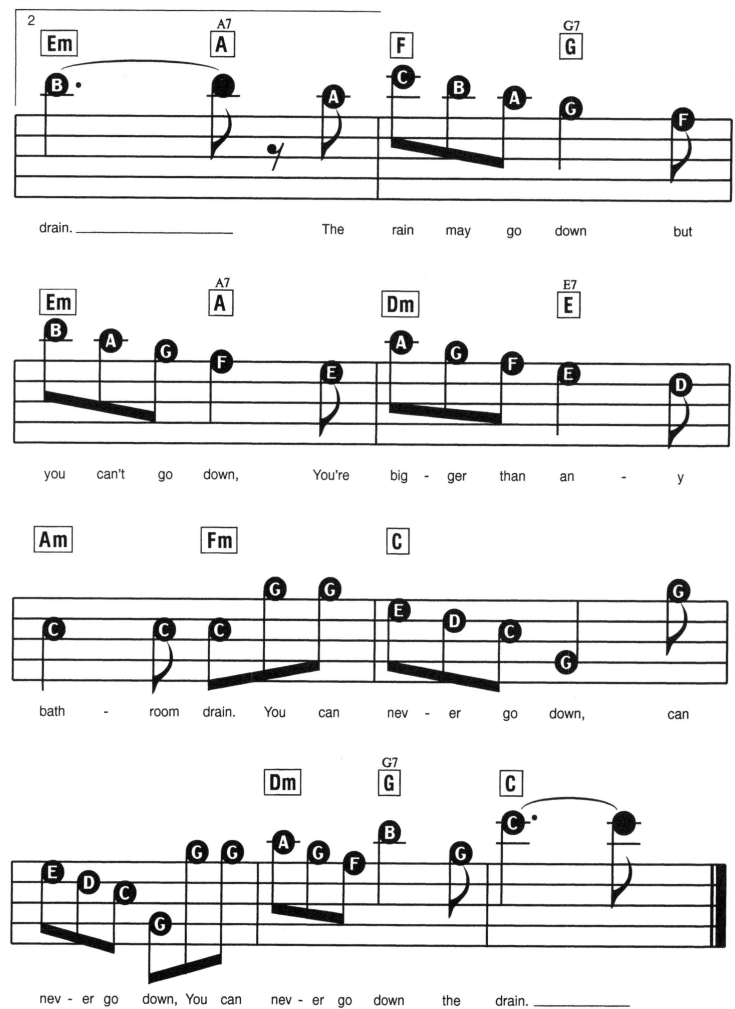

You're Growing

Registration 9
Rhythm: 8-Beat or Rock

Words and Music by
Fred Rogers

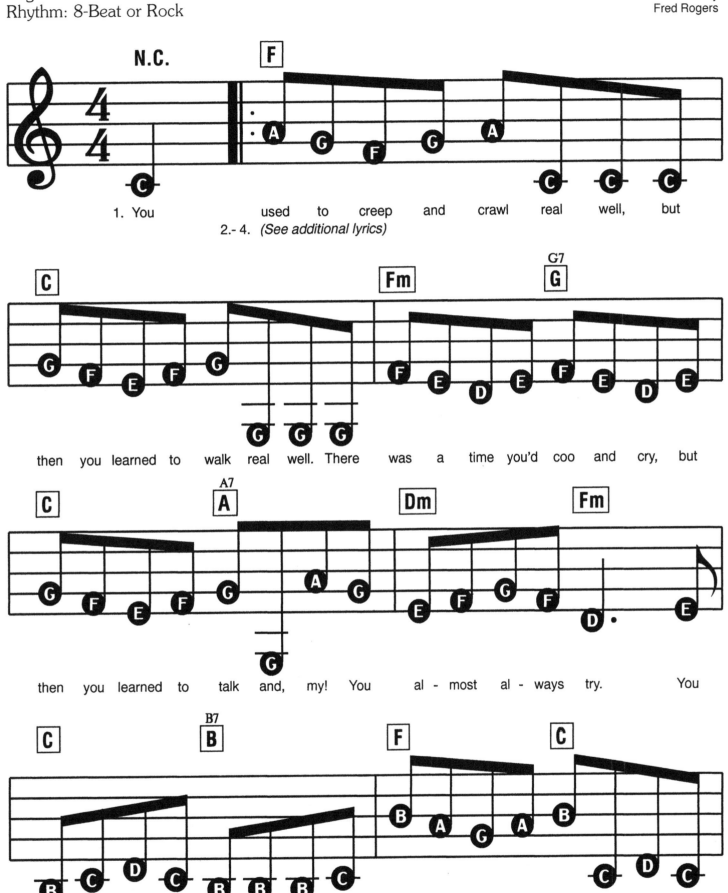

52

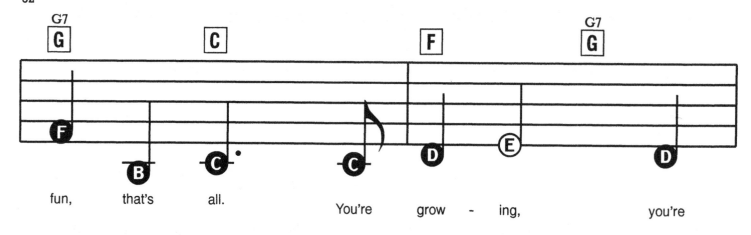

fun,   that's   all.   You're   grow - ing,   you're

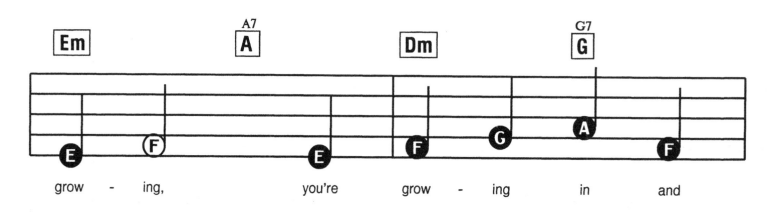

grow - ing,   you're   grow - ing   in   and

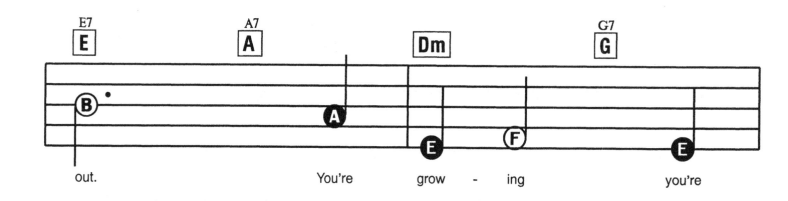

out.   You're   grow - ing   you're

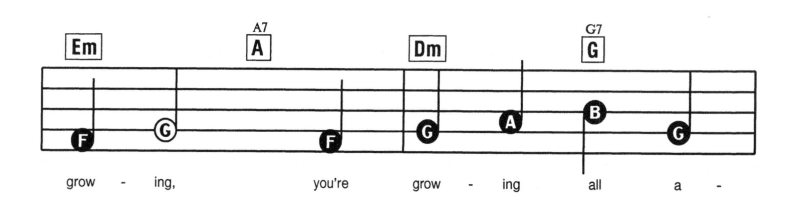

grow - ing,   you're   grow - ing   all   a -

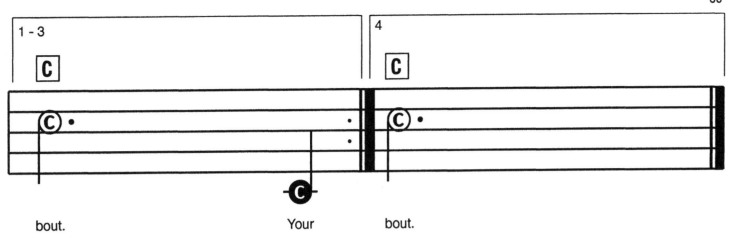

bout.   Your   bout.

Additional Lyrics

2. Your hands are getting bigger now.
   Your arms and legs are longer now.
   You even sense your insides grow
   When Mom and Dad refuse you so...
   You're learning how to wait now.
   It's great to hope and wait somehow.
   I like the way you're growing up.
   It's fun, that's all.

   Chorus:

   You're growing; you're growing;
   You're growing in and out.
   You're growing; you're growing;
   You're growing all about.

3. Your friends are getting better now.
   They're better every day somehow.
   You used to stay at home to play,
   But now you even play away.
   You do important things now,
   Your friends and you do big things now.
   I like the way you're growing up.
   It's fun, that's all.
   Chorus

4. Someday you'll be a grown-up too
   And have some children grow up too.
   Then you can love them in and out
   And tell them stories all about
   The times when you were their size;
   The times when you found great surprise
   In growing up. And they will sing,
   It's fun, that's all.
   Chorus

You've Got to Do It

Registration 7
Rhythm: Swing or Shuffle

Words and Music by
Fred Rogers

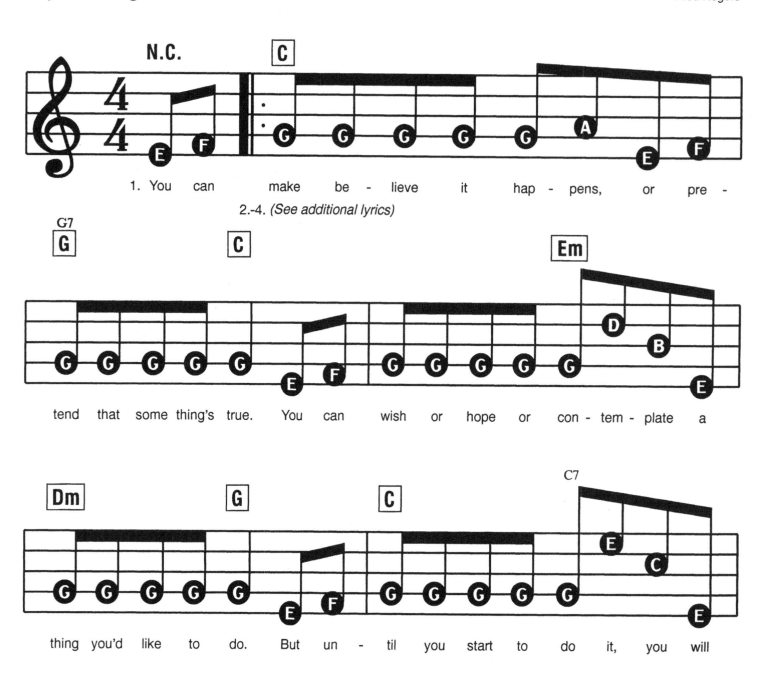

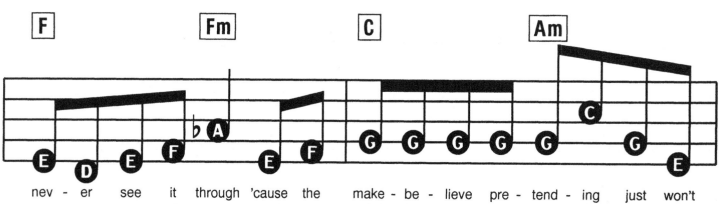

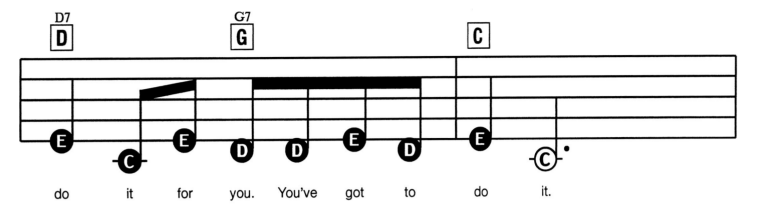

do it for you. You've got to do it.

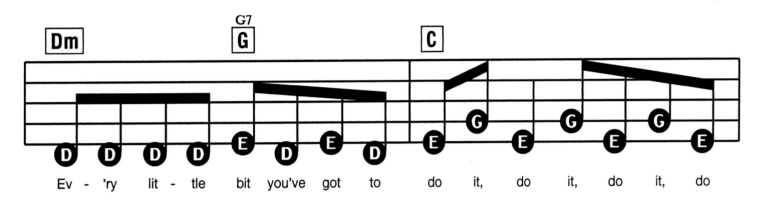

Ev - 'ry lit - tle bit you've got to do it, do it, do it, do

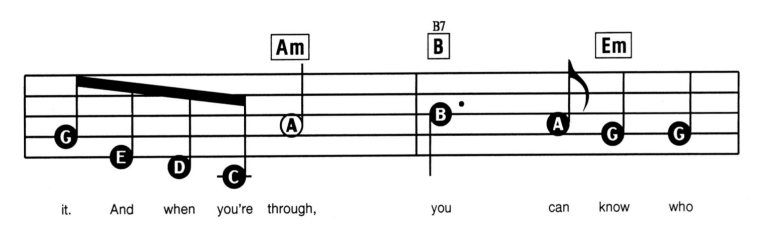

it. And when you're through, you can know who

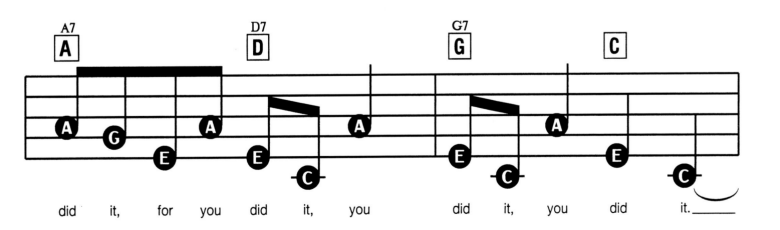

did it, for you did it, you did it, you did it._____

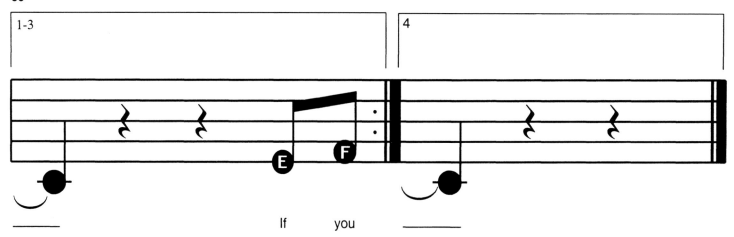

If   you

Additional Lyrics

2. If you want to ride a bicycle and ride it straight and tall.
   You can't simply sit and look at it
   'Cause it won't move at all.
   But it's you who have to try it, and it's you
   who have to fall (sometimes)
   If you want to ride a bicycle and ride it straight and tall.

   Chorus:

   You've got to do it
   Every little bit, you've got to do it, do it, do it, do it,
   And when you're through, you can know who did it
   For you did it, you did it, you did it.

3. If you want to read a reading book
   and read the real words too,
   You can't simply sit and ask
   the words to read themselves to you.
   But you have to ask a person
   who can show you one or two
   If you want to read a reading book
   and read the real words too.
   Chorus

4. It's not easy to keep trying,
   but it's one good way to grow.
   It's not easy to keep learning,
   but I know that this is so:
   When you've tried and learned
   you're bigger than you were a day ago.
   It's not easy to keep trying,
   but it's one way to grow.
   Chorus